Where Christianity Went Wrong, When, and What You Can Do

Where Christianity Went Wrong, When, and What You Can Do About It

Patricia A. Williams

Library of Congress Number: 2001118152

ISBN #: Softcover 1-4010-2192-1

Photo of author by Nick Nichols.

This book was printed in the United States of America.
To order additional copies of this book, contact:
Xlibris Corporation
1-888-7-XLIBRIS
www.Xlibris.com
Orders@Xlibris.com

To the Jesus scholars and historians of the two first centuries,
without whom this book would never have been written.

Contents

Acknowledgments

I would like to thank the Biblical Archaeology Society for maintaining my interest in the historical Jesus and Jay Worrall, Beth S. Neman, Rem Edwards, and Maggie Potts for reading the entire manuscript and making such helpful suggestions. Xlibris has been very helpful in seeing the manuscript into print. Mistakes and infelicities are my own.

I can be contacted by email at theologyauthor@ aol.com or through my website at http://hometown.aol.com/theologyauthor/myhomepage/index.html which also contains information on my other books.

BEGINNINGS

This book is about the transformation of the historical Jesus into two different Jewish Messiahs, the Greek *logos,* and the divine Roman Emperor. It suggests Christians give up the Jewish, Greek, and Roman concepts of Jesus to embrace the message and mission of the man. To imitate the historical Jesus would be to worship him truly.

But I must begin at the beginning. Chapter 1 is about how I came to write this book and about the book itself. Chapter 2 provides a brief cultural and historical overview of the two first centuries—1 BCE (B.C.) and 1 CE (A.D.)—and relevant events before and after them. This information will help the reader understand where Christianity went wrong and why.

1 Getting Acquainted

Inspiration

Recent scholarship on allusions to Roman culture in the New Testament inspired this book. Thomas Schmidt's article on the Roman imperial procession in Mark's passion narrative caught my attention first. Schmidt made me see Mark differently. Before, he had seemed a dullard. Suddenly, he was a genius. Not long after, the Jesus scholar N. T. Wright gave a talk in Charlottesville, Virginia, on the Roman background to Paul's letters. Wright and Schmidt together made me see the New Testament differently. Their work revivified my long-term interest in the historical Jesus.

The search for the historical Jesus captures many of my enthusiasms. I am a philosopher of science. Like most philosophers of science, I am familiar with issues of evidence and theory formation. These are central issues in historical Jesus studies. My specialty is the theory of evolution. My knowledge of the theory of evolution shapes the suggestions for thinking about Jesus in Chapter 11. I focus on the theory's implications for human nature and ethics. This focus led me to publish a book on Original Sin (Williams 2001). For vacations, I often attend Biblical Archaeology Society seminars, many of which have been on the historical Jesus and related material, such as the Dead Sea Scrolls. All these interests have influenced this book.

Other Christians have influenced it, too. They have long puzzled me. I think being a Christian means to follow Jesus. Other Christians seem to believe it means following Calvin, Luther, or the Pope, all of whom think quite differently from Jesus. Prominent Christians such as Pat Robertson, Oral Roberts, Bob Jones, and the Bakers built financial empires. The Papacy and monastic orders in the Roman Catholic Church also have extensive financial holdings. Yet Jesus owned almost nothing, castigated the rich for their hard-heartedness, and suggested that God's empire is worth all a person possesses. Why do these Christians ignore Jesus?

Moreover, I did not seem to fit very well into the Episcopal culture in which I grew up. I had different values from other Episcopalians. Many valued money and status. Jesus valued neither, and I tried to listen to Jesus. I remember a woman who lived in the most stylish place in Charlottesville complaining one summer Sunday after church that the water in her country club's pool was too warm, and she would have to drive some distance to a spring-fed pool so she could enjoy swimming. I thought of the kids in the inner cities where the tarmac melts under foot. Jesus asks us to shun egocentricity and show compassion. This woman thought of nothing but herself, and then in a petty and superficial way.

Yet Christians who take the Bible more seriously than Episcopalians are not much different. They praise the Bible and insist on taking it literally or inerrantly, but they do not seem to care much about Jesus. Instead, they worry about their own sin, the sins of others, and their salvation after death. Something seems wrong. Thomas Schmidt and N. T. Wright helped me see what is wrong, when it went wrong, and what to do about it. The solutions to all three problems depend on understanding the historical Jesus and realizing how belief in his resurrection influences his Jewish and Gentile followers.

Faith

Christians place their faith in all sorts of things. Some have faith in the Bible, others in the Pope, still others in their church. I never had much faith in any of these things. I could see the Bible is not infallible because it has internal contradictions, both in the Hebrew Scriptures and in the New Testament. I did not understand why the Pope should be any more infallible than I am, which is a scary thought. I hoped the bishops of my church would occasionally do what I thought was right, but I did not count on it. This turned out to be wise.

I discovered that my faith lay in my experiences of God and Jesus. I met Jesus in church regularly through the celebration of the Last Supper in churches of all sorts, from charismatic to Roman Catholic. I also met him at odd, unexpected times elsewhere. I claim I would know him if he were to walk down the street.

As a result, I have not had to have faith in an inerrant Bible or Pope, church, minister, priest, or guru. I have not needed to believe in an empty tomb to believe in the resurrection because I have known the resurrected Jesus. As discussed in Chapter 5, Paul finds himself in much the same position. He never knew of an empty tomb and could not have cared less. He had something better. He knew Jesus, raised from the dead.

One of the wonderful things about the scholarly search for the historical Jesus is that the seeker lives with Jesus while on that search. Although different in significant ways, the historical Jesus, man of flesh and blood, and the resurrected Jesus, spirit (however embodied) of that man, are not as different as might be thought. I think they are not so different because the spirit of the man still lives. Jesus still loves with compassion and forgives as he did in the first century. To learn more about the historical Jesus is to find out more about the resurrected Jesus whom we can know now. This is a book about the historical Jesus and how knowing about him can affect our lives.

The Jews' story

The first section of Chapter 2 tells the history of the Jews, briefly, as it is given in the Hebrew Scriptures and, when these cease, primarily in Josephus, the first century Jewish historian. I have added some very traditional, very round dates to convey the sweep of time involved. I make no effort to follow modern biblical scholarship here. These sections are interested in the Jews' story as Jews of the two first centuries saw it, not as modern scholars do.

The rounded dates are easy to remember—2000 for Abraham, 1000 for David, 1 for Jesus. This lends the story a slightly mythological flavor, a flavor most modern historians think deserved. The first date many modern historians will claim as certain is 722, the Assyrian defeat of the northern empire of the Jews. After 722, the dates given are historical, not so round, and not so easy to remember. The historical Jesus is born in the year 6 or 4 "before Christ," that is, before the more mythological, more easily remembered date.

About this book

Although I have tried to tell the Jews' story as Jews of the two first centuries would have known it, I have used modern scholarship to portray the historical Jesus. I have attempted to give the clearest, soundest, and fairest summary of contemporary scholarship on Jesus that I can present briefly. It is found in the section entitled "Jesus." Since there are thousands of articles and myriad books on the historical Jesus from contemporary scholars, I have left out a lot. Most notably, I often do not present the scholars' arguments for their conclusions. For these, I recommend the scholars themselves. Many have written very readable books. I have listed those I have used under "Works Consulted" at the end of this book.

I am not a professional Jesus scholar. Much in this book depends heavily on the work of contemporary Jesus scholars and the historians of the two first centuries, to whom this book is dedicated and without whom it would never have been written. However, current Jesus scholarship has four shortcomings I have had to address.

The first shortcoming is the lack of consensus. Few Jesus scholars have attempted to build a consensus among themselves, for they are interested in developing their own, unique portraits of Jesus. The Jesus Seminar is an outstanding exception, and the scholars in it are to be congratulated for working together so well, so diligently, and to such impressive effect. Although indebted to the Jesus Seminar, the construction of the consensus in this book is my own and original. Others might do it differently.

The second shortcoming is that Jesus scholars are divided on one crucial issue, which is the central problem in Jesus scholarship today. The crucial issue is whether Jesus is primarily a prophet of the end time or primarily a reformer. Which side scholars take on this issue colors the rest of each one's portrait of Jesus. Therefore, I need to arrive at my own conclusion. In Chapter 6, I use the scholars' work to develop an original argument whose conclusion is that Jesus is a reformer who mocks the Jewish dream of the end time. My conclusion makes sense of the evidence both groups of scholars use to support their respective positions and throws light on other issues as well.

The third shortcoming is that Jesus scholars do not ask what Jesus considers sinful. It is perfectly clear that he thinks the usual list of sins, like stealing, murder, and adultery, sinful. Yet I argue, the sin Jesus denounces repeatedly is the condemnation and exclusion of others, a sin that arises from arrogant belief in one's own righteousness. It is the predominant sin of his time among the Jews, leading to murderous factionalism. Moreover, I argue that Jesus sees everyone as sinful and in need of God's mercy, himself included. He considers the failure to recognize one's own sinfulness to be a devastating kind of blindness.

My presentation of the scholarly consensus combined with my solution to the central problem in Jesus scholarship and my discussion of Jesus on sin provide an unusually robust and coherent picture of Jesus. My portrait accounts for most of the evidence we have about Jesus and shows that Jesus' preaching on sin concentrates on the primary problem of Jews in his era. factionalism. Thus, my portrait makes Jesus very much a Jew of his time. This is what a sound portrait of Jesus should do.

Fourth, most scholars have no interest in applying the results of their scholarship to our lives today. In contrast, I think the conclusions scholars reach have important implications for our lives. Our beliefs are involved. Given what we know of the historical Jesus and the cultures around him, we should reject some foundational Christian doctrines, for they come not from Jesus but from Jewish and pagan culture. Our behavior is also involved. Given what we know of the historical Jesus, we need to examine our lives and, perhaps, change them, if we wish to follow Jesus. This book suggests some directions for change.

Everyone who works on the historical Jesus must distinguish between the two first centuries. I have used contemporary notation to make the distinction. BCE is the former BC, "before Christ." and CE the former AD "Anno Domini," in the year of the Lord. BCE stands for "Before the Common Era" and CE is "Common Era." The contemporary notation complements the contemporary scholarship. It says nothing about my own beliefs.

In discussing the Gospels, I have written as if someone named Mark wrote Mark, etc. This is shorthand almost everyone uses. At the same time, almost everyone knows that anonymous people wrote the Gospels, the names having been added to them long after their composition. I see no point in making an issue of this.

For Christian groups early in the first century CE, I speak of "assemblies" rather than "churches." This is for the sake of accuracy. The early Christian groups were unstructured assemblies, often disagreeing with each other. The institutional structure and unity implied by "church" had not yet developed.

There is only one Greek word for the regimes translated into English as "kingdom" and "empire." Usually, the duality of the English results in the kingdom of God and the empire of Rome. The distinction in English is unwarranted and makes it difficult to understand why the kingdom of God should frighten the empire of Rome. But in Greek, the empire of God is contending with the empire of Rome. Suddenly, the issue acquires a different hue. Because the similarity between one understanding of the empire of God and the ancient concept of the empire of Rome is an important theme in this book, I have used "empire" for both "empire" and "kingdom." This retains the original Greek usage and emphasizes the conflict between the two empires.

I have used the New Revised Standard Version of the Bible (NRSV) wherever I have quoted directly from the text. Although it is not my favorite, it seems the most broadly acceptable translation. For well-known and easily located passages, I have not cluttered the text with citations. Every reader should already know that the narratives about Jesus' birth occur at the beginning of the Gospels in which they appear, the passion narratives close to the end, and the post-resurrection appearances at the end. When I have used citations, I give them in standard form, for example, the First Letter to the Corinthians, chapter 15, verse 17 is 1 Cor 15:17. References to half verses use *a* and *b*, that is, 1 Cor 15:17a refers to the first half of verse 17, 17b to the second half.

I have not cited Gospel parallels (similar passages in more than one Gospel). The curious reader can find the canonical parallels in almost any scholarly Bible. Robert Funk and the Jesus Seminar's *The Five Gospels* and *The Acts of Jesus* both cite parallels from non-canonical sources.

This book has three related purposes. They are (1) to offer a coherent portrait of the historical Jesus in agreement with most historical Jesus scholars while solving problems that divide them, (2) to show how and why Jesus' followers distorted his message, and (3) to apply these insights to lives today, both religious and secular. In brief, the book concludes that people should discard the distortions and imitate the historical Jesus. It continues with a brief overview of the history and culture of the two first centuries.

2 *The Two First Centuries*

Jewish empire

The Jewish empire begins with God's call to Abraham about 2000 BCE to leave his home and travel to the land God promises him. Abraham reaches the land, but sojourns there as an alien, for the Canaanites already live there. Abraham's posterity leave the land during a famine and go to Egypt where the Egyptians enslave them.

About 1300, God calls Moses to lead the Jews out of slavery, and he brings them across the Red Sea into the desert beyond. This escape is the Exodus, celebrated by Jews everywhere as Passover, the joyous annual festival of Jewish liberation.

After forty years in the desert, where God gives Moses laws for the Jews, the Jews finally reach the land God promised them. This time, they conquer it and establish a confederation of twelve tribes ruled by judges. Because the Jews are divided into twelve tribes, they have difficulty defeating the enemies on their borders and soon ask God for an emperor to unite them. The prophet Samuel anoints David emperor in about 1000 BCE. David unites the tribes, and they defeat their enemies and conquer Jerusalem, which David makes the capitol of the empire.

All Jewish emperors are anointed, and because "Messiah" means "anointed," all are Messiahs, whether good or bad. However, the Jews come to think of David as special, for he turns out to be the greatest emperor they ever have. Traditions of his military prowess, his love of God, and God's love for him, influence later Jewish thought.

David centralizes worship in Jerusalem. His son, Solomon, builds God a Temple there.

After Solomon dies, the empire splits into north and south. In 722, the northern empire falls to the Assyrians who deport the ten tribes living there, and they disappear. The vanished tribes become know as "the ten lost tribes of Israel."

In 586 BCE, the Babylonians under Nebuchadnezzar conquer the south. The Babylonians take the leaders and many of the people to Babylon. The period they remain captive is called the "Babylonian Captivity" or the "Exile."

The Exile lasts until 538 when the Persians under Cyrus the Great defeat the Babylonians. The Jews return to their own land to reconstruct Jerusalem and rebuild the Temple. Ezra brings a copy of the laws God has given the Jews for daily living and worship. The laws are in the five books of Torah, which later become the first five books of the Christian Old Testament. Thus begins the "Second Temple Period," which lasts until the Romans destroy the Temple in 70 CE.

This history of exile and return, slavery and freedom, affects Jewish thinking. It leads the Jews to believe that God is faithful and will eventually redeem them from exile and slavery. This is not because they are remarkably good, but because God loves them and is faithful.

Why, then, have they suffered so? They conclude that they suffer when they fail to follow the spirit of the Torah as they pursue gain by exploiting the poor, and they fail to keep the letter of the Torah in their worship. Eventually, they conclude, God chastises them through earthly agents like Nebuchadnezzar. God sends other earthly agents like Moses, David, and Cyrus to redeem them.

When the Jews return to their land and rebuild the Temple, they are still under Persian domination. Rarely again do they gain complete independence. In 334 BCE, Alexander the Great of Macedonia begins the occupation of Asia Minor. His armies conquer the Holy Land and eventually reach all the way to Egypt and India, spreading Greek language and culture as they go.

Some Jews living in the Holy Land want to adopt Greek culture, but others object, claiming that to adopt Greek ways is to contravene God's laws. When added to existing factionalism and shear lust for power, this disagreement erupts into civil war. Antiochus IV Epiphanes intervenes in 169 BCE, occupies Jerusalem, and sets up an altar to the Greek god Zeus in the Temple. Jewish tradition ever after refers to this incident as "the abomination of desolation."

Moved by anger and piety, a year later a Jewish family named Maccabbee leads a revolt. The revolt is successful. The Maccabbees purify the Temple and rededicate it in 164. They finally establish complete Jewish independence in 141 BCE. They also reconquer much of the old Davidic Empire and, as they do, they force the non-Jewish inhabitants to convert or drive them out of the land. Jewish exclusiveness and intolerance lead many Greek-speaking people to despise them as arrogant and misanthropic.

Jewish tradition soon claims that the Maccabbean revolt succeeds because of the family's piety. For two centuries thereafter, many Jews believe they can defeat their foes if only they have pious armies like the Maccabbean forces, led by devout men like David.

Not long after independence, civil war begins again. Each faction foolishly courts Roman help. In 63 BCE, the Romans invade and conquer the Holy Land. Once again, the Jews are under foreign domination. This is the situation when Jesus is born.

For the next two centuries, various Jews mount revolts against Rome, believing God will help them. Several revolts occur under Pontius Pilate, Roman ruler of part of the Holy Land from 26 to 36 CE, a ruler insensitive to Jewish traditions and unusually brutal. One revolt occurs when Pilate brings Roman standards bearing pictures of emperors into Jerusalem. The Romans worship emperors as gods. The Jews are deeply offended by having what they consider idols in their holy city, and they stage a sit-down strike until Pilate removes the standards. Later, Pilate tries to take money from the Temple treasury for civil construction, and the Jews protest again.

In 66 Eleazar, son of the high priest, leads a revolt of the Jewish aristocrats against Rome. He suspends the sacrifices for the emperor and Rome that have been offered daily in the Temple. In the Roman Empire, this amounts to a declaration of war. Soon the lower classes join the revolt. They attack the Romans, but they also strike the aristocrats, looting their homes and murdering the inhabitants. Despite this outbreak of civil war, the rebellious Jewish forces manage to hold Jerusalem until 70 when the Roman general Titus defeats them and burns Jerusalem and the Temple. A final rebellion under bar Kochba in 132 sees the complete destruction of Jerusalem and its replacement with a Roman city from which Jews are barred. The two first centuries are not peaceful times for Jews. Mostly this is because the Jews are divided into ferocious factions.

Jewish factions

There are a variety of Jewish factions in the two first centuries. The New Testament mentions three: the Samaritans, Pharisees, and Sadducees. The Samaritans separate from other Jews centuries before Jesus. They claim to be the true keepers of Torah, and their Torah says Mt. Gerizim is the only proper place to worship. They build a temple there in the fourth century BCE that the Maccabbees destroy in 128 BCE. They have their own priesthood, calendar, and purity laws. The other Jews despise them, not only as religiously corrupt, but also as ethnically impure.

The Pharisees are the liberals of their day. They are lay people who follow Torah, but add oral law to it, which they treat as equal to the Torah. They bring to Judaism belief in the resurrection of the dead. They are active in the synagogues and popular with ordinary people. However, the aristocratic conservatives hate them. One such leader, Alexander Jannaeus, crucifies hundreds of Pharisees outside the gates of Jerusalem. After the Romans destroy the Temple, the Pharisees are the only significant faction remaining. Present-day Rabbinic Judaism springs from them.

The Sadducees are priests who rule the Temple. Because the Temple functions somewhat like a central bank, they have access to a great deal of money and also profit from Temple sacrifices, of which they receive a portion. Partly because they are wealthy aristocrats themselves, they collaborate with the powerful. After the Roman conquest, they join forces with Rome. Numerous Jews consider this collaboration treason, and the militants mark Sadducees for assassination. When Rome destroys the Temple, they cease to exist, for their occupation is gone.

Also conservative are the Essenes, authors and collectors of the Dead Sea Scrolls. The Essenes consist of several groups, some married, some celibate, some living in the desert, others in cities. They follow Torah and establish their own elaborate rules for living in community. Because their calendar differs from the calendar used at the Temple and they consider the Temple priesthood illegitimate, they do not celebrate the Temple festivals. Yet they are not against the Temple as an institution. They want to take it over and purify it.

The Pharisees are the Essenes' most detested enemies. This is partly because the Essenes and Pharisees think alike. They both believe those who follow Torah are righteous and those who do not are sinners, that the righteous will be saved and sinners condemned. However, they interpret Torah differently. Their differences must have been particularly galling to the Essenes, for the Essenes' leaders are priests, whereas the Pharisees are lay people. The Essenes must feel that the Pharisees are stealing their prerogatives. The Pharisees' popularity with the populace would not have soothed the wound.

The Essenes believe they are living very near the end of time when God will send a Messiah to war against the Romans and all the unrighteous, and they plan to join the battle. In 68 CE, the Romans annihilate those Essenes living in the desert, and the movement collapses.

Zealots and Sicarii do not wait for God's intervention before taking up arms. Zealots are among those who seize the Temple when civil war comes in 66. The Sicarii at the Temple battle the priestly aristocrats, then flee to the fortress at Masada, which falls to the Romans in 73, the Sicarii having committed mass suicide rather than surrender. Their name comes from a dagger called a *sica* they use to assassinate Jews who collaborate with Rome.

Beliefs about the end time motivate many of the more militant groups. These beliefs draw on Jewish traditions. Just as the Jews had been redeemed from slavery in Egypt and exile in Babylon, so they will be redeemed now, for God will again intervene. God will raise up another Messiah like David and warriors like the Maccabbees, zealous for God's Torah, and restore the Jews to their former glory.

Once, the hope of restoration had been a historical hope that the Jews would return to their land to prosper as an independent nation. During the two first centuries, this hope becomes a dream. The dream tells of the restoration of the Jews at the end of time. A cosmic war between good and evil will precede the restoration. God, God's angels, and the Messiah, along with one's own faction, will fight the devil, the Romans, and the other factions. In the end, the righteous will be vindicated, the unrighteous vanquished. The righteous are those who keep Torah law. Each faction keeps it differently.

The dream includes an idealized end time of peace and prosperity when weeds and thorns will be no more, and predators become vegetarians. All the dispersed Jews will be united in a glorified Jerusalem. Those who believe in the resurrection of the dead feel certain that the righteous dead will join them, and the original twelve tribes return. Then, the Gentiles will recognize the Jews as God's people, pay tribute to them, and worship God in a splendid Temple sent from heaven. The dream of Jewish restoration dies almost exactly a century after Jesus, in the bar Kochba rebellion which suffers defeat in 135. For almost two thousand years thereafter, the Jews concentrate on religion, leaving politics and conquest to others.

God-fearers are the final group that might be classified as Jewish. The God-fearers are Gentiles who participate in synagogue worship, join Jewish prayer groups, and adhere to many Jewish laws and customs. However, they do not convert to Judaism. They continue to participate in pagan worship and sacrifices, shun circumcision, and keep only selected laws. When a new Jewish faction arises that offers full membership to the uncircumcised and sets aside Torah demands, many convert. Thus, the new Jewish faction becomes predominantly Gentile within a generation of its founding. Later, it takes the name "Christian" and separates from Judaism.

Each Jewish faction thinks it possesses God's true word, knows God's true will, and is doing God's will. Each is proud of its righteousness, meaning each is proud it follows the Torah the right way, which is God's way—in truth, only the faction's way. Each persecutes the other. When Alexander Jannaeus is in power, he crucifies Pharisees. When the Pharisees achieve power, they remove the Sadducees from their political offices and persecute, exile, and murder Essenes. The Maccabbees destroy the Samaritan temple. Samaritans harass Galilean pilgrims who pass through Samaria on their way to Jerusalem. Militant members of factions assassinate their enemies. The Holy Land is a hotbed of righteousness and hatred. Some of that hatred is aimed toward Rome, but never enough to unite the factions against their common enemy. The belief that one's own faction is righteous and all others unrighteous is tearing Judaism apart.

Roman Empire

Rome begins as a city-state. Unlike the Greek city-states, it extends citizenship to freed slaves and to residents of other cities. Thus, Rome expands rapidly, and as it does, it absorbs foreign practices, ideas, and cults, especially those from Greece. It even has a ceremony for adopting others' gods. Roman soldiers entice enemy gods to their own side by promising them more honor and worship than their enemies give them, if they will fight for Rome. Given the extent of Rome's victories, many gods must have heard and heeded!

As Rome extends its rule to Spain, Gaul, Britain, North Africa, Macedonia, and Syria, it becomes unstable. In 133 BCE a series of social and political upheavals occurs, culminating in civil war in 90. The civil war ends at the battle of Actium in 31 BCE when Octavian defeats Antony and Cleopatra and brings Egypt, the last Greek Empire, into the Roman fold.

In 27, the Roman senate passes a decree giving Octavian the title "Augustus." He is the first, the highest, the most august citizen of Rome. His status matters enormously, for Roman social and economic relationships depend on the patronage system.

The patronage system is a complex of unequal social relationships based on debt and repayment, beneficence and acknowledgment, gift and gratitude. In a series of patron-client relationships that extends in an ever expanding and descending hierarchy throughout the Roman empire, Augustus is the primary patron, a generous giver of gifts. He has many to give. He offers titles, positions, and offices. He gives his soldiers money and land. He gives the poor housing and food. He builds roads, founds cities, and rebuilds Rome.

Under the patronage system, these gifts are not free. Every recipient is expected to return something, if only loyalty and gratitude. The rich repay by erecting public works dedicated to Augustus and by remembering him in their wills. Over time, the result of this system is to concentrate the wealth of Rome in a few families and to leave the common people destitute and dependent on the largess of the emperor and other patrons. It is a system built on inequality, flattery, and exploitation, and it functions in the Holy Land as elsewhere under Roman rule. When Jesus shows partiality for the poor and suggests the difficulty of the rich attaining salvation, this is the system he is protesting. This same system helps spread the cult of the emperor to every city and square in the empire.

Roman religion

Augustus Caesar is Julius Caesar's adopted son. In his lifetime, Julius seeks recognition as a god, which is one reason his enemies assassinate him. By doing so, they turn him into a martyr. When a comet (called a star, then) is sighted during games held in his honor after his death, the viewers are certain that it signals (or is) the ascent of his soul to the realm of the gods. Julius has arrived. There is now no doubt of his divinity. The star becomes a popular sign of the divine. The Gospel of Matthew (2:2) places one at Jesus' birth.

Because his father is a god, Augustus is the son of a god. His official name becomes "*Imperator Caesar divi filius.*" Translated, this is "Emperor Caesar [his surname], son of god." Augustus also is honored with other titles. The most common (in order) are savior, benefactor, creator, and liberator. Gaining the office of *pontifex maximus* gives him an additional title, high priest. These are titles the New Testament applies to the risen Jesus.

Augustus' forty-five year reign leaves an indelible stamp on Rome. He is the recipient of a cult that becomes the most widespread in the empire. To have a cult means to be honored with games, images, shrines, temples, priests, sacrifices, and processions. Under the patronage system, cultic activities and structures dedicated to Augustus multiply rapidly. Provinces, cities, groups, and individuals compete with each other for the best games, grandest temples, most magnificent buildings, longest processions, and most splendid sacrifices. Cities mint coins in honor of Augustus and carve statues to him. Many celebrate their New Year's Day on Augustus' birthday. Romans proclaim that a new age dawned with the advent of Augustus.

In Asia Minor, where Christianity will find its home among the Gentiles as it never does among the Jews, there are more than eighty temples dedicated to the emperors, most to Augustus. Architects redesign city centers to accommodate the cult. Ephesus, where Paul lives for at least two years, is one such city.

In Ephesus, there are four temples erected or dedicated to Augustus, plus an altar, a portico, four gymnasia, several civic buildings, gates, and many statues. As in many cities of the empire, a person cannot go anywhere in public without being reminded of Augustus' deification. Even the mileposts along the roads between cities bear inscriptions to him. He paid for many of the roads.

As emperors succeed one another, the images on coins, pictures, and statues change. These changes influence clothing styles and hairstyles throughout the empire. The presence of the emperor, son of god, is pervasive everywhere, including Galilee with its Roman cities of Tiberius and Sepphoris, the latter only four miles from Nazareth.

As far as we know, the cult does not influence Jesus, but it influences the authors of the New Testament. Paul comes from Tarsus in Asia Minor. His native language is Greek. He uses the Greek translation of the Hebrew Scriptures. Mark and Luke are Gentiles, clearly more familiar with Greek traditions than Jewish ones. John, although a Jewish Christian, is angrily alienated from Judaism. Even Matthew seems more at ease in the Greek city-states than he does in Palestine and Jerusalem. The cult of Augustus is part of the air they breathe. As we now know, it deeply influences Paul's letters and the Gospels.

Especially influential is the imperial procession, at the end of which the emperor is deified. The procession begins in a courtyard with the emperor dressed in purple, a color reserved for royalty and divinity alike, with a crown of laurels on his head. Soldiers shout his praise. The procession then winds through the streets of Rome with the emperor carried in a chariot and the crowd clamoring to witness the epiphany of a god. At the end, the procession stops, and the emperor is offered a cup of wine, which he refuses. In his passion narrative, Mark applies all these imperial details to Jesus. Chapter 8 deals at length with the parallels and their meaning. Here, the point is merely to highlight the influence the cult of the emperor has on the Gospels.

The imperial cult constitutes the religion of the common people. The religion of Greek philosophers is also familiar to the Greek-speaking populations of the two first centuries.

Plato (427-347 BCE), one of the greatest of the Greek philosophers, holds a very high conception of God as perfectly good. Being perfect, God could not have created this imperfect world. Plato thinks an intermediary must have created it. Meanwhile, Stoic philosophers propose a creative force they call the "*logos*." These similar concepts merge by the two first centuries into the *logos* who organizes the world according to divine law.

Plato also posits a realm of ideas existing from eternity. These ideas are more or less synonymous with generic terms like "tree" or "house" or "squirrel" (as contrasted to particular trees, houses, or squirrels), but Plato claims for the generic terms a real and separate existence.

Many Jews of the two first centuries familiar with Greek philosophical religion try to reconcile it with Judaism. The Septuagint assists them. The Septuagint is the Greek translation of the Hebrew Scriptures, believed to be divinely inspired, available in full by the beginning of the two first centuries. The Septuagint often translates Hebrew ideas into Greek idiom. For example, when God speaks to Moses from the burning bush (Exod

3:14), the Hebrew which is translated into English as "I am who I am," becomes in Greek/English, "the Being." This is Plato's term. Thus, the Septuagint itself does much to reconcile Greek and Hebrew concepts.

The greatest philosopher to attempt further reconciliation is Philo of Alexandria (~20 BCE-~50 CE). Both Paul and John's Gospel refer to Christ as the *logos*, which is one of Philo's central concepts. Philo finds Plato's God who exists from eternity compatible with the God of Hebrew Scripture. However, he does not think Plato's ideas exist from eternity, for only God is eternal. Instead, Philo suggests that the ideas begin as thoughts of God, with God creating them later as separate existences placed in the *logos*. Philo equates the *logos* with God's creative word in Genesis 1 and Psalm 33:9, "For he [the Lord, meaning God] spoke [his *logos*], and it came to be:/ he commanded [with his *logos*], and it stood firm." Christians later interpret the passages of Scripture referring to "the Lord" as references to Jesus. Thus, John can begin his Gospel, "In the beginning was the *logos*" and have *logos* refer to Jesus.

JESUS

The next three chapters are about Jesus. Chapter 3 addresses the question of why readers of the New Testament need scholarship in order to understand the Jesus who lives in Galilee and dies outside Jerusalem's walls. Chapter 4 summarizes the best modern scholarship on the historical Jesus. Chapter 5 discusses the resurrection. These chapters help us understand Jesus. They also mark the path his followers should have taken.

3 *Scholarship on Jesus*

Scholarship

What "scholarship" means is not always clear, especially in biblical studies and inquiries about Jesus. For the purposes of this book, scholarship means research by trained historians, biblical scholars, and theologians, but only if they begin their research without knowing what conclusions they will reach. Such people try to get as close to the truth about Jesus' life and death as they can, but they are aware that truth is often elusive, and they know they might fail or only partially succeed.

Scholars may be contrasted with apologists, scholarship with apologetics. Apologists begin research already knowing the conclusions they will reach because they already know what the truth is, a truth usually given them by their particular Christian denominations. They do research in order to show others that the truth they already have can be derived from the relevant materials, usually the Scriptures. At its worst, apologetics descends to proof-texting, the practice often used by the preachers who frequent the mass media, that is, quoting verses of the Bible out of context to support a dubious position.

This book presents the best contemporary scholarship on Jesus without referring to apologetics. The materials listed under "Works Consulted" are scholarly. Therefore, the conclusions reached here about Jesus do not necessarily agree with the views of any particular Christian denomination.

Another distinction may also be helpful, that between history and piety. Readers can consider the Bible from more than one perspective. They may use it for pious purposes, seeking God, perhaps prayerfully, in its pages. Generations have used it in this manner. However, the Bible can also be treated more objectively and critically. A reader may ask whether Luke makes any historical mistakes. Finding historical errors in the Bible decreases its usefulness as history, but does not change its status as a sacred text through which God may speak to us. In other words, the Bible's scientific or historical accuracy does not affect its sacred status or its excellence as a work enhancing piety.

This book is interested in history rather than piety. It wants to know about Jesus, the person who lives in Galilee and dies outside Jerusalem about 33 CE.

The Gospels as history

Merely a careless and superficial reading of the Gospels shows that the first three are remarkably similar. Because they are similar, scholars refer to them as the "synoptic Gospels," meaning that they "see together" and give similar portraits of Jesus.

In the synoptics, Jesus speaks in short, pithy, sometimes very funny sayings, filled with wild exaggerations like someone's eye having a log in it and camels going through needles' eyes. Jesus also reverses social expectations, justifying tax collectors and condemning Pharisees. Jesus rarely speaks about himself, but he says a lot about the empire of God. His mission takes one year. At the Last Supper, Jesus blesses the bread and wine.

The fourth Gospel is different. In it, Jesus gives long speeches about himself and says things like "I am the bread of life," "I am the true vine," "I am the way, the truth, and the life." Jesus' mission takes three years. At the Last Supper Jesus washes his disciples' feet. He does not bless the bread and wine.

The synoptics and John disagree with each other over many other details—how often Jesus goes to Jerusalem, the date of the Last Supper, Jesus' reaction to his own death. The disagreements mean they cannot both tell the true history of Jesus. Either he did or did not wash his disciples' feet at the Last Supper. Either he spoke most of the time in short, pithy sayings or else he delivered long discourses. Scholars have had to decide which tradition represents Jesus more accurately. They have reached a very broad consensus on this issue, deciding that the synoptics give a more accurate historical portrait of Jesus than the Gospel of John.

This does not mean pious Christians should throw out John's Gospel! John's Gospel is a wonderful spiritual work, richer than the synoptics. Written late, about 90, it tells of the early assemblies' experience of the risen Jesus. The assemblies believe he is the bread of life, the true vine, the way, truth, and life. This is the way early Christians in John's tradition honor Jesus.

Disagreements also occur among the synoptic Gospels. Of the three Gospels, Matthew and Luke have narratives about the birth of Jesus (Mark begins with Jesus' baptism). Matthew has Joseph and Mary travel from Bethlehem to Egypt to Nazareth. In Luke, they go from Nazareth to Bethlehem to Jerusalem and back to Nazareth. Matthew has them on the road because they are afraid Herod is trying to kill their son, then because they want to avoid settling in Herod's son's territory. In Luke, they travel to Bethlehem because of a census taken when Quirinius is governor of Syria, go to Jerusalem for Jesus' circumcision, and return home. Because the sequence of events and the motivations are different, at least one of these narratives does not tell the true history of Jesus' parents' travels just before and after his birth.

Luke has Jesus born when Herod the Great rules Judea and Quirinius is governor of Syria. However, Herod dies in 4 BCE, and Quirinius does not take office until 6 CE. Luke cannot be right about the rulers in office when Jesus is born.

Problems like these call for scholarship to sort them out. Once the evidence is sifted, it turns out that Jesus is probably born in Herod's reign, about 6 to 4 BCE. Matthew and Luke write the birth narratives to make theological points about Jesus, to help Christians understand who Matthew and Luke think Jesus is. Probably neither narrative is historical, but both have served Christian piety for 2000 years. Discrepancies among the Gospels are not the only problems. Scholars must also confront a record made after Jesus' death and deal with the question of sources.

The record

In explaining the history of the Jews and some cultural aspects of Greek and Roman life, Chapter 2 attempts to close the gap between Jesus' culture and ours. Here, I mention obvious differences that influence our understanding of the Gospels.

In Jesus' time, there are no camcorders, no tape recorders, no news reporters, and no news media. No one records Jesus' exact words. Even if someone had, he spoke Aramaic, whereas all the Gospels are in Greek. The Gospels do not contain Jesus' exact words. Furthermore, in the first century there are no pencils, no pens, no paper, no books, and no mass literacy. It is an oral culture, with little need to chronicle in writing what people say and do. While he is alive, no one writes down Jesus' words or records his deeds.

In Jesus' time there are no machines. Power is muscle power. News travels on foot, by donkey and horse, and by boats that hug the seacoast due to the lack of navigational equipment and fear of storms. The best pace of travel for most people (with the exception of professional couriers) is about twenty miles a day, ten miles an average day's distance. News travels slowly, mouth to mouth. Sometimes, people hear it incorrectly, forget part of it before they pass it on, or exaggerate bits and pieces to catch the attention of the next listener. This is how stories about Jesus' words and deeds travel in Galilee, in Jerusalem, and finally in the Roman towns of the Jewish Diaspora.

Beliefs about Jesus impede the literate from chronicling his life. While he is alive, there is no need to write about him, for he is present. His followers believe his resurrection is a sign that he will return immediately. No need to write about him, for this generation is the last. After his return is delayed and after the Romans destroy Jerusalem in 70 CE, someone in the second generation after Jesus' death composes the first Gospel. The author composes with the expectation that Jerusalem's destruction is now the sign of Jesus' immediate return. This Gospel, later attributed to Mark, is in the present tense in Greek, with constant use of the word "immediately." Time hurries on. No time to write a lot, at leisure. Barely time to get the story down at all.

Thus, a gap exists between Jesus and the Gospels. Jesus speaks Aramaic, the Gospel writers Greek. The Gospels appear after the destruction of Jerusalem, an event of enormous cultural and religious significance for Jews, the end of a way of life and worship practiced for a thousand years. Jerusalem's devastation and the destruction of the Temple need explanation. People living after the destruction, including the authors of the Gospels, interpret events in the light of that dissolution, seeing God's hand in it. Moreover, at least two of the Gospel writers, Mark and Luke, are Gentile. Jewish culture is foreign to them, especially that of the Second Temple Holy Land. Matthew's heritage is uncertain, but he is not familiar with the geography and practices of the Holy Land. John's culture is Jewish, but he is a Christian Jew of the Diaspora who is excluded from the synagogues. He is angry with Jews and Judaism. His anger gives him an agenda. The other Gospel writers have agendas of their own.

The sources

Scholars who have studied the Gospels think the synoptics "see together" because they have common sources. Mark is one source. Both Matthew and Luke, writing during the third generation after Jesus' death, around 80 CE, quote from Mark, borrow stories from him, and paraphrase his words. Matthew fairly consistently keeps to the order of events in Mark. Both derive their passion narratives from Mark. Deeds and sayings common to Mark and Luke or Mark and Matthew have only one source, Mark.

Mark is the shortest Gospel, more filled with deeds than sayings. Luke and Matthew are longer, and their Gospels are replete with those short, pithy sayings of Jesus. Some of the sayings in Matthew and Luke that are not found in Mark are alike, word for word. Others are surprisingly similar. Scholars posit another source for these sayings, a gospel of sayings designated "Q" after the German word for "source," collected shortly before Mark is written. Sayings absent from Mark but common to Matthew and Luke have only one source, Q.

In addition, Matthew and Luke contain material unique to their respective Gospels. For example, only Matthew compares God's empire to a fishing expedition (13:47-59) and only he has Jesus claim to have been sent exclusively to lost Jews (15:24). Only Luke tells the story of the Good Samaritan (10:30-35) and the parable of the Prodigal Son (15:11-32). These unique materials have separate, single sources that scholars call M or L, respectively.

Being so different from the synoptics, John has drawn on a separate tradition. However, he may have known the other Gospels, or one of them. Much of his passion narrative is similar to those in the synoptics and may depend on one of them.

The earliest source for scholars' knowledge of Jesus is Paul, who writes during the 50s, close to the death of Jesus and before the destruction of the Temple. But for two reasons, Paul's letters do not disclose the historical Jesus as well as might have been thought from the dates of his writing. First, Paul is a Greek-speaking Roman citizen of the Diaspora, cultured in the ways of Rome, although trained as a Pharisee. Jesus is an Aramaic-speaking Jew from the Holy Land, with little of Rome in his background, and not a friend of Pharisees. Jesus and Paul think differently.

Second, Paul evinces no interest in Jesus' life, neither his deeds nor his sayings. This is because Paul believes he has his own, private, revelation(s) directly from the resurrected Jesus. Paul's gospel is not similar to the Gospels. Paul's gospel is of Jesus' descent from heaven, death, and ascent back to heaven. In Paul, the historical Jesus, man of Galilee, preacher of the empire of God, disappears. Paul is not much help to scholars who seek to paint an accurate portrait of the life of Jesus.

4 The Life of Jesus

Events most certain

Scholars are absolutely certain that a person named Jesus of Nazareth once existed. They think three things about his life are certain to be historical. The first is his baptism by John the Baptist. This event is certain because the existence (and death) of John the Baptist is attested from a separate, secular source, Josephus' *Antiquities of the Jews*. Jesus' baptism is also recorded in more than one Gospel source, yet his baptism by John is an embarrassment to the early Jesus movement, which exists in rivalry to John's. That John baptizes Jesus suggests that John is superior to Jesus. Groups do not publicly chronicle events embarrassing to themselves unless those events are so widely known that not to record them would look like falsification.

The second certain event in Jesus' life is his crucifixion. Again, Josephus offers extra-biblical evidence, again the crucifixion is in more than one Gospel source, and again it is an embarrassment to Jewish expectations, which are of a militant, victorious Messiah rather than a person executed as a common criminal.

Third, scholars are sure Jesus dies during the rule of Pontius Pilate, a Roman governor notoriously insensitive to Jewish traditions and so brutal that Rome finally relieves him of duty. Because these three things about Jesus' life are so clearly true, they must be included and accounted for in any accurate portrait of the historical Jesus.

Immediately below is a more complete outline of Jesus' life that a scholarly consensus speaks of as certain, but not absolutely certain, to be historical.

Scholars are almost certain that Jesus is born around 4 BCE, near the end of the reign of Herod the Great. Being a Jewish child, he is circumcised on the eighth day, then grows up in Galilee, in the town of Nazareth, with a mother named Mary, four brothers, and a number of sisters. He becomes a disciple of John the Baptist and is baptized by him, but does not join him. Instead, he returns to Galilee and becomes an itinerant exorcist, healer, and preacher who speaks about God's empire. Before long, crowds come to hear him, and he calls twelve disciples. His mission in Galilee lasts from one to three years.

Sometime around the year 33, Jesus travels from Galilee to Jerusalem for the annual Passover festival, when other pilgrims also flock to the city. There, he causes a stir in the Temple that angers and/or frightens the Temple authorities. Not wanting trouble in crowded Jerusalem, they arrest him and take him to Pilate, the Roman governor, as a dangerous pretender to Jewish leadership. Pilate has him crucified. Sometime later, Jesus' once frightened followers believe they experience him as resurrected and begin speaking boldly of his resurrection to people in the streets and synagogues.

Scholars who have researched the life of Jesus feel fairly certain that all these events happened. In any accurate reconstruction of Jesus' life, they, too, must be included and explained. The three sections below offer a still more complete account of Jesus' life, but the new details have somewhat less historical probability than those already mentioned. Nonetheless, the new details are hardly in the category of things recounted in the Gospels that scholars are certain did not happen. (They have made lists of those, too.)

Jesus and John the Baptist

Jesus grows up in Nazareth, but John does not baptize him until he is more than thirty years old. In first century culture, this makes him at least a middle-aged man, old enough to have been a grandfather. No one knows what he is doing from the time he reaches manhood at about age thirteen until he is seen with John, a period of some fifteen or twenty years. Nor does anyone know what John has been doing until his baptizing days.

Yet there are clues. All the Gospels depict John as having the words of Isaiah on his lips, "The voice of one crying out in the wilderness:/Prepare the way of the Lord, make his paths straight" (Mark 1:3). As scholars now know from the Dead Sea Scrolls, which were discovered in caves above the Dead Sea between 1946/47 and 1956, this passage from Isaiah might be called the mission statement of the Essenes. Moreover, the scrolls are found close to where John is preaching, near a desert community of Essenes.

There are other similarities between John the Baptist and the Essenes. The Essenes think the Temple is corrupt, so they do not sacrifice there. John announces forgiveness of sins outside the Temple system, without requiring sacrifice. Both John and the Essenes believe the end time is arriving very soon, and they warn of God's wrathful judgment then.

John and the Essenes also practice ritual bathing, but here the similarities end. The Essenes bathe themselves repeatedly in specially designed and dedicated pools to maintain ritual purity. Once people repent and join the community, they follow Torah as the Essenes interpret it, so they are righteous by definition. In the end time, they think, God will save the righteous. They do not need to bathe in repentance of sin.

In contrast, John baptizes others, apparently each person only once. He immerses those who seek baptism in flowing water as a symbol of their repentance. At the end time, he preaches,

God will save those who repent and turn to righteousness. Whether he thinks the righteous also need to repent is not clear, but he must have been aware that each Jewish faction defined righteousness differently.

It is possible that John started his career as an Essene, then broke away from the community to begin his own mission as a prophet and baptizer. Scholars do not think Jesus was ever an Essene. However, he is deeply influenced by John the Baptist and is familiar with Essene beliefs.

In any case, John baptizes Jesus with his baptism of repentance. Jesus seems to undergo a profound religious experience at this time, an experience so powerful he feels compelled to go alone into the desert to consider what has happened to him. When he returns, he does not rejoin John. Instead, he goes back to his home district and begins his own mission. It appears that his experience at his baptism is a life-transforming event.

Jesus in Galilee

Jesus does not return to his home village, but establishes his base further north in Capernaum on the sea of Galilee, from which he travels without possessions as an itinerant healer, exorcist, and preacher. Josephus calls him, "a doer of wonderful works" (*Antiquities*, III.3). There is good evidence that he relieves Peter's mother-in-law of a fever, heals a skin disease resembling leprosy, and cures paralysis, blindness, and a hemorrhage. He may also have performed what appeared to be resuscitations, although the Gospel accounts of these deeds resemble very closely similar stories in the Septuagint and may have been borrowed from it.

Jesus also practices exorcism, as do others in his day. To be an exorcist requires a person to consort with demons, and it is difficult for bystanders to know which power the exorcist is commanding, the divine or the demonic. Scholars are fairly certain that Jesus is accused of being an agent of demons. In his culture, this is roughly the equivalent of being insane. A passage in Mark (3:21) has his family try to restrain him because they consider him out of his mind.

People in Jesus' day believe illness and demon possession are punishments for sin. For Jesus to heal these maladies is the equivalent of his proclaiming that God has forgiven the sins of the sick and possessed, as the Gospels make abundantly clear. Thus his "wonderful works" carry one of John the Baptist's central messages, the forgiveness of sins, but without requiring baptism.

Jesus' family is not among his followers. The incident of their trying to remove him from the crowds because they think him mad is followed in Mark by his refusing to see them when they ask for him and, instead, declaring his followers his family. Moreover, his hometown rejects his mission. Had he received support from his family, his hometown might have been more accommodating.

Some of the religious authorities oppose his mission as well, and with reason. Jesus and his followers do not observe the social precepts of their culture. Jesus consorts with social misfits and outcasts and, worse yet, eats with them, a colossal breach of propriety in Jesus' day when a man sought to dine only with equals and superiors. Rather than fasting in the accustomed fashion once or twice a week, Jesus holds banquets where he and his followers consume enough food and wine to give Jesus the reputation of being glutton and a drunkard.

Jewish men do not speak to women in public in Jesus' day, but Jesus publicly consorts with women. They are in the crowds that follow him. At least one touches him in public, hoping to be healed. Women of means support his ministry. They are among his staunchest early followers and probably stand by him later, at his crucifixion. If, as John 4:1-43 recounts, he speaks to a woman in Samaria, he commits a double breach of social etiquette, for socially conscious Jews shun Samatarians.

Occasionally, Jesus breaks the Sabbath. More often, he jettisons the purity laws that provide the rules for daily living, laws controlling how and what to eat, when and how to bathe, how to wash cooking vessels, and how to treat corpses, among other things.

The purity laws are not merely an aggregation of regulations. They have two main purposes. One is to separate the holy from the profane. A related purpose is to separate society into distinct social castes with clearly defined boundaries. To eat with social inferiors and to break the purity laws is to destroy those boundaries, to invite social chaos. As it is, there is more than enough social chaos in Galilee—too many Jewish factions, too much sheer anarchy, crime, and banditry. In this context, breaking the purity laws must have seemed more like madness than mere perversity.

Jesus also calls twelve disciples, mostly local fishermen, but perhaps also a Zealot or Sicarius, a scribe, and a tax collector. On the whole, this is not a notable group of men, this inner circle around Jesus. Moreover, Jesus memorably calls twelve, a number with deep resonance in the end time dream of Jewish separatists and rebels, a number representing the twelve tribes of Israel, tribes to be restored to their rightful place after holy and devastating war. That Jesus is known to lead such a group must have made those around him question either his sanity or his peaceful intentions, or both. Jesus' deeds in Galilee suggest that he is playing a dangerous game.

Jesus' words do not diminish this impression. They fit his deeds, a sign of his sanity and integrity. Mostly, he talks about God's empire. This subject is in keeping with his number of disciples. God's empire will come, and the twelve tribes will be reconstituted. Nonetheless, the Gospels and other materials about Jesus do not suggest he is ready to take up arms and usher in the empire himself. The fact that he is the only one of his circle crucified implies that the Romans do not consider his movement dangerous. If they imagine a movement menacing, they do not hesitate to execute all its members.

Jesus characterizes God's empire in unexpected ways. He compares it to a mustard seed (Mark 4:31), proverbial for its insignificance. He compares it to yeast. Yeast is also tiny, in the sense that a trivial amount in comparison with the flour is sufficient to make bread rise. And Jesus speaks of the yeast as "hidden" (Matt 13:33) in the flour, much as a seed is hidden in the ground before it sprouts. (The translation of the NRSV alters the original Greek to read "mixed in with.") God's empire is like a pearl (Matt 13:45), a small jewel easily hidden, but worth all else a person possesses—or like a treasure concealed in a field (Matt 13:44), again hidden and small, but worth everything else a person has. This empire does not come with great signs, like stars falling from heaven. War does not herald its coming. It is already here, diminutive and unnoticed, but ready to grow many times its present size, worth all a person has now, in this life.

God's empire is also like a banquet (Luke 14:16-24) to which the invited guests refuse to come because they are busy with other interests, so the poor, lame, and blind are invited, instead.

Some very fine scholars of Jesus think he preaches publicly about the imminent end time dream imagined by Jewish factions like the Zealots and Essenes and Jesus' mentor, John the Baptist. Other equally fine scholars think he does not preach about the imminent end time. Whether or not some kind of end-time prophecy is central to Jesus' message is the main issue dividing Jesus scholars today. Chapter 6 addresses this controversy.

Connected with Jesus' messages about God's empire is a second theme, God's forgiveness and compassion. Perhaps the most famous story Jesus tells is the story of the Prodigal Son. The Prodigal Son wastes all his inheritance in wantonness and abandons his religion to herd pigs, yet is embraced by a father moved to compassion, who runs to meet him upon his return, dresses him in fine clothes, and gives him a banquet (Luke 15:11-31) envied by his elder brother. Such is God, who blesses the hungry, grieving, and poor (Luke 6:20-22), sends rain on the righteous and unrighteous (Matt 5:45), and gives to those who ask (Luke 11:9).

Jesus expects people to behave accordingly. He asks people to love their enemies as well as their friends (Matt 5:44).

Jesus does not think everyone who encounters God's empire will embrace it. The mustard seed grows into a weed that might be thought evil, in need of uprooting. Yeast is an unclean food removed from Jewish households during Passover. God's empire is like a landowner (Matt 20:1-15) whose generosity some people envy, just as the elder brother in the parable of the Prodigal Son envies his father's generosity. Evidently, some people who encounter God's empire dislike it.

Jesus is not always positive. The entire saying about loving enemies is "'You have heard that it was said, "You shall love your neighbor and hate your enemy." But I say to you, Love your enemies and pray for those who persecute you.'" The counsel to hate enemies is not in the Hebrew Scriptures. It is Essene. Jesus is deliberately condemning Essene morality, as he also does when he says that the sabboth is made for human beings (Mark 2:27) and breaks sabboth observance by healing in cases that are not emergencies. Of course, given the antipathy among the factions in the Holy Land and the Jews' hatred of the Romans, Jesus' advice to love enemies extends beyond the Essenes even to love of Romans.

Jesus condemns ties of kinship, so important to Jew, Roman, and Greek alike. He speaks of his followers as his kin, in deliberate rejection of his own nuclear family (Mark 3:33-35).

Jesus denounces divorce (Mark 10:2-9). In doing so, he enhances the status and welfare of Jewish women in his day. Under Jewish law, a man could divorce a woman, but a woman could not divorce her husband. Some Jewish traditions made divorce very easy, so a man could treat his wife like tattered merchandise. Moreover, women depended financially on men, and divorce frequently left women destitute. Forbidding divorce protected women.

Jesus does not encourage public prayer and fasting. He recommends praying alone in one's room (Matt 6:6). He deliberately seeks solitude in deserts and on mountains to pray, sometimes literally sneaking away from his disciples to do so. Maybe he needs a quiet place where he can listen to God.

He repeatedly condemns the rich and those who practice social exclusion (often the same people), telling stories about banquets that the better sort refuse to attend, but the poor and outcast enjoy instead (Luke 14:16-24). He also tells of a good Samaritan (Luke 10:30-35), a contradiction in terms to Jews who hate Samaritans as ethnic and religious inferiors. That Jesus heals the sick and possessed, people considered unclean and unacceptable to God, carries a similar message of inclusion.

In judging the righteous and the sinner, Jesus often reverses the stereotypes of his day. The large majority of Jews admire the Pharisees, for they keep strict rules and are experts in Torah. In contrast, the majority hate tax collectors as extortionists and traitors. Jesus tells of an exemplary Pharisee and a repentant tax collector (Luke 18:10-14), then commends the tax collector rather than the Pharisee. Chapter 7 explores the meaning of this parable.

Jesus behaves similarly when he forgives a woman's flagrant adultery (John 8:3-11), pointing out that those who condemn her are themselves sinners. For the most part, scholars do not consider John's Gospel historical. However, this story is not part of John's original Gospel. It is absent from the earliest manuscripts, floats from place to place in later ones, and does not reflect John's style. Yet the story is well attested by some of the best historians and soundest documents of early Christianity. Furthermore, it sounds like Jesus. Something like it may well have happened.

Jesus equates God's empire with something small and hidden, here and now, with compassion, banqueting, love of enemies, inclusiveness, the forgiveness of sins, and the salvation of sinners. He calls for loosening or breaking kinship ties. He is an itinerant.

living without possessions. Although some scholars think Jesus preaches of the dream of the end time, his themes differ markedly from those of the dream. In the dream, the righteous are vindicated while their enemies, the unrighteous, are destroyed. Kinship ties are reconstituted when the twelve tribes of Israel gather once more. The Jews repossess the land and grow wealthy from Gentile tribute. Jesus is upsetting peoples' expectations. His words in Galilee are as hazardous as his deeds.

Jesus in Jerusalem

As far as Jesus scholars can ascertain, the words and deeds of Jesus in Jerusalem have only one source, Mark. This makes it very difficult to distinguish between the authentic Jesus and Mark. Unfortunately, Mark's perspective is not Jesus'. Mark is a Gentile writing to Gentiles who lives a generation after Jesus and knows about the destruction of the Temple. Thus, he has a threefold different perspective from Jesus. Moreover, many details in Mark's Jerusalem narrative have parallels in the Septuagint. It is possible that Jesus was deliberately trying to fulfill the Hebrew Scriptures, but not the details peculiar to the Septuagint. More likely, whoever has written whatever materials Mark is using, and Mark himself, search the Septuagint to find out about Jesus. Because Jesus' second-generation followers believe Jesus' words and acts fulfill the Scriptures, their searching the Scriptures to find out what he did and said makes sense. They probably see themselves as filling in details not available from other sources, not as writing fiction to present as history. These facts warrant historical caution, and even skepticism, about the Gospels' portrait of Jesus in Jerusalem.

Thus, very few scholars think Jesus rides into Jerusalem on a donkey because the scene comes directly from Zechariah 9:9 and Psalm 118:25-26. On the other hand, almost all suppose Jesus causes a commotion in the Temple while engaging in symbolic actions there. Prophets in the Hebrew Scriptures also make symbolic gestures in the Temple. Exactly what Jesus does, and why, are deeply contested. Sections of chapters 6 and 9 explore this issue further.

Necessarily, Jesus and his followers eat a last supper. They eat together often, and because Jesus dies, there must have been a final meal. Yet the synoptics and John disagree about the day of the last meal, so it is difficult to ascertain what it means. John compounds the difficulty by telling of Jesus' washing his disciples' feet while leaving out the blessing of the bread and wine. Jewish and Roman hosts alike commonly bless the food and the wine at meals, so Jesus probably says the blessings. Yet how to interpret the words of blessing is contested. Certainly, it is possible that Jesus connects the blessings with his own death. He understands human psychology, so he must realize his deeds and words provoke the enmity of many.

Almost every scholar is certain that the Temple authorities arrest Jesus, most likely because of the incident in the Temple, perhaps because crowds hail him as the Davidic Messiah who will restore Jewish independence, perhaps also because of his earlier behavior in Galilee. Clearly, the authorities turn him over to Rome, for he dies by crucifixion, Rome's form of execution for rebels and the poor. Jesus fits both categories. Whether the Romans give him a trial is uncertain. Pilate, the Roman governor, is notoriously brutal, known for executing people without properly trying them. He might simply have had Jesus executed at the request of the Temple authorities who have collaborated with the Romans for years to keep the peace in Jerusalem.

Certainly, Jesus is crucified outside the walls of Jerusalem. Probably he is flogged first, as is Roman custom. Roman practice is to keep friends and relatives away from the crosses, and the Gospels confirm either that none of Jesus' followers is there or that a few women watch from a distance. Almost everything the Gospels claim happens during the crucifixion has parallels in the Hebrew Scriptures. Again, those who developed the Gospel material probably searched the Septuagint for appropriate passages to tell them what happened, for they believed that Jesus' words and actions fulfill the Scriptures.

Roman practice is to leave the bodies on the crosses for dogs and vultures to eat, a warning to other aspiring rebels and bandits, an insult to the person and his family. Sometimes, the Romans bury the crucified in shallow, unmarked, mass graves. On the other hand, Josephus tells of having three of his friends removed from crosses (*Life* .75), so removal of crucified bodies is not unknown. Most scholars admit they do not know what happens to Jesus' body. Among those who claim to know, opinions differ.

The resurrection is sufficiently complex to require a separate chapter. Suffice it to say here that some of Jesus' disciples, Jesus' brother James, and the Saul who is to become Paul, believe God raises Jesus from the dead and risk their lives to say so.

5 The Resurrection

Beliefs about the dead

There is nothing distinctive in Jewish beliefs about the dead. Whatever a group of Jews believes, a group of Gentiles also believes. Because the Pharisees triumph over other Jewish factions after 70 CE, belief in the resurrection of the dead becomes one of the defining beliefs of later Judaism. But in the two first centuries, it is the belief of only one faction of Jews.

The least a person can believe about life after death is that there is none. In early Judaism, this is the prevalent belief, and it survives until the disappearance of the Sadducees after 70. It is also a Roman belief, common enough to produce a number of tomb inscriptions that are variations on, "I was not, I was, I am not."

To believe more, but not much more, is to believe that everyone has a shadowy existence after death, a nondescript continuance, often compared to that of a shade or a mist. Such a death is grim, but it happens to everyone. It has nothing to do with rewards and punishments. Some Jews and Greeks and Romans hold such a belief.

A more robust belief is to think that everyone is naturally mortal, but the righteous live on after death supernaturally while the wicked perish. Again, some groups of Gentiles and some groups of Jews hold this belief. It is fairly common among the Maccabbean rebels.

A still richer belief is that everyone is naturally immortal. This is Plato, but it also appears to be the belief of the Essenes. The Essenes think the wicked suffer torments, while the righteous enjoy happiness. Plato believes in a version of reincarnation. Some first century Jews seem also to believe in reincarnation. Their believing in reincarnation makes sense of the questions asked of John and Jesus, whether they are prophets of old returned (Matt 16:14; John 1:21, 25).

Some Jews believe in bodily resurrection. Among them are those who believe that only the righteous are resurrected, while the wicked remain dead. Others believe everyone is resurrected, and the righteous enjoy happiness while the wicked suffer.

Those who believe in resurrection disagree about what kind of body is resurrected. Some believe that this once mortal body of flesh and bone returns. With this belief comes the opinion that resurrected life resembles mortal life, except that it is filled with peace, prosperity, and joy. This position is easy to mock, as the Sadducees do in Luke 20:27-33 when they ask Jesus about seven brothers who successively marry the same woman, whose wife will she be?

Expressing a belief that life after resurrection will not be like the old, earthly life, nor the resurrected body built of flesh and bone, Jesus replies in a fairly well-attested passage that, in the resurrection, marriage will be no more, for the resurrected resemble angels (Mark 12:25). In Jewish angelology, angels are immortal, spiritual beings, without substantial bodies, and without sexual differentiation, immortals not needing to reproduce.

Paul on resurrection

As a young man, Paul is trained as a Pharisee and, presumably, shares the Pharisees' belief in the resurrection of the dead. At his conversion, Paul believes he encounters the resurrected Jesus, but he says little about his encounter, and what he does say has him transported to paradise, "whether in the body or out of the body, I do not know" (2 Cor 12:2). Luke gives three accounts of Paul's conversion, but these are Luke's creation. Luke does not appear to know Paul's letters, here or elsewhere. If nothing else, Paul's encounter must have confirmed his belief that people can be resurrected.

Paul's fullest account of resurrection takes up the whole of 1 Corinthians 15. He speaks first of the information he has received about Jesus from the disciples. Jesus, he says, was buried, resurrected, and appeared to various disciples singly and in groups, to Jesus' brother James, and, finally, to Paul himself.

Paul goes on to argue that there must be a resurrection of the dead because Jesus has been raised. If there is no resurrection at all, Jesus could not have been raised. Jesus is the first of many to be resurrected as well as the representative of those to be raised, just as the first fruits taken to the Temple are both first and represent the entire harvest.

The other people to experience resurrection will be those who belong to Jesus, the dead first, then the living (1 Thess 4:16). Only those belonging to Jesus are to be resurrected. Those who do not put on Christ will die and remain dead. Apparently, Paul does not believe the wicked will suffer punishments after death.

Then, Paul addresses the issue of resurrected bodies. He says that the present, fleshly body dies. Its burial is like the sowing of a seed. From it arises a heavenly body such as God chooses to give. That body is spiritual. It is imperishable. "Flesh and blood cannot inherit the kingdom of God…we [who are alive at the final resurrection] will all be changed…this perishable body must put on imperishability" (1 Cor 15:50-53).

This passage seems perfectly clear, and it fits with the passage in Mark where Jesus says the resurrected will not marry, but be like angels. Resurrected bodies are not flesh and blood. The flesh and blood body dies. From it as a kind of seed, resurrected, spiritual, imperishable bodies arise. Paul does not believe in the resurrection of the flesh. He knows nothing of an empty tomb. He believes in the resurrection of the dead, a spiritual resurrection and a glorified body, given by God. Such a glorified body he has already confronted, he believes, in his conversion encounter with Jesus.

Paul's is the earliest account in the canonical Christian literature of the resurrection of the dead. The Gospels are later than Paul. They have a more ambiguous story to tell.

The Gospels on Jesus' resurrection

All the Gospels tell of an empty tomb. Three contain narratives of post-resurrection appearances. However, the stories differ.

Mark, the earliest, has Mary Magdalene, Mary the mother of James, and Salome go to the tomb to put spices on the body. When they arrive, the stone covering the entrance to the tomb has been rolled away. A young man in the tomb who is dressed in white tells them Jesus has been raised and will meet the disciples in Galilee. The women flee in terror, telling no one. Mark does not record any resurrection appearances. (The appearance vignettes in Mark are not part of the original Gospel.)

Matthew—with Mark in front of him—says Mary Magdalene and the other Mary come to see the tomb. An earthquake shakes the ground as an angel in white descends from heaven and rolls the stone away. Guards posted by the Temple authorities faint. The angel says Jesus has been raised and to tell the disciples he will meet them in Galilee. Jesus then immediately appears to the women. He also tells them he will meet the disciples in Galilee. Meanwhile, the guards report back to the Jewish leaders who bribe them to lie and say someone stole the body. Jesus appears to the disciples once, on a mountain in Galilee, and sends them to make disciples of all nations.

Luke—also with Mark in front of him—says some unnamed women come with spices, find the stone rolled away, and Jesus gone. Two men in dazzling clothes appear. The women are frightened. The men tell them Jesus has risen, and they go back and tell everyone, but the disciples are skeptical. Peter looks into the tomb and is amazed.

In Luke's account of post-resurrection events, Jesus appears twice, first to two disciples on the road to Emmaus and then to all the disciples in an unspecified place in Jerusalem. In both cases, Jesus reviews the Scriptures for them, demonstrating that they foretell his dying and rising. In the Jerusalem scene, the disciples think Jesus is a ghost, so he shows them his scars and eats some fish to assure them he is not. He tells them to stay in Jerusalem until given power from heaven. Jesus then leads them to Bethany where he ascends to heaven. In Luke's second volume, Acts, the power from heaven arrives, like fire, and the disciples speak in tongues (Acts 2:3-4).

Perhaps with all three Gospels beside him, John has Mary Magdalene approach the tomb alone, see that the stone has been removed, and run back to tell Peter and John. She tells them someone stole the body. Peter and John run to the tomb. John arrives first and sees the body wrappings. Peter enters the tomb first, with John close behind. John believes first. (John's Gospel evinces much concern about priority among the disciples.)

Now, the story of Mary Magdalene continues. She is weeping at the tomb when two angels in white appear. A brief conversation ensues, then Jesus appears. She does not recognize him until he speaks to her. He tells her he is ascending, and she leaves and tells the disciples. Later, with the disciples behind locked doors in Jerusalem, Jesus appears. He shows them his scars, breathes on them, and gives them the Holy Spirit, an action that makes the tongues of fire in Acts unnecessary and redundant. A week later, with the disciples again in the room, door shut, Jesus reappears. Thomas, who had been absent the first time Jesus appeared in the room, had not believed the other disciples, so Jesus tells him to touch the scars, and Thomas believes.

In a separate ending attached to John, Jesus appears to the disciples in Galilee. They have returned to their old occupation of fishing. In a scene reminiscent of the calling of the disciples, Jesus tells the luckless fishermen to fish on the other side of the boat, where they get a huge catch. Peter then recognizes Jesus and jumps into the water to reach him quickly. They all eat breakfast together on shore.

Again, Jesus appears to Peter and John and makes a somewhat ambiguous statement with the possible implication that John will not die until Jesus comes back. A rumor to this effect spreads in the community, but the author assures the reader that the statement need not be understood this way.

What is to be made of all this variation? Mostly, the variation shows that the Gospels are not written in a vacuum, but address a culture responding to followers of Jesus who proclaim his resurrection. There is a dialogue going on, but the Gospels only present half of it, the believers' half.

Scholars think it well attested that Jesus' disciples flee when he is arrested. The earliest tradition of post-resurrection appearances has Jesus appear to his disciples in Galilee. Thus, in the earliest Gospels, men or angels or Jesus say Jesus will meet the disciples in Galilee. Adding these two pieces of information together, scholars think Jesus' disciples flee in dismay and confusion at Jesus' arrest and crucifixion and go home to hide and recuperate. Hopes crushed, they take up their old occupations, mostly as fishermen. It is in Galilee that Peter and some other disciples come to believe they have experienced the resurrected Jesus.

The earliest believers' report is Paul's. Paul is certain Jesus has been raised. He sees Jesus himself, resurrected, and he knows the disciples' tradition that Jesus appears to them various times after his death and burial, singly and in groups. Paul does not need an empty tomb. Nor need he report that the first appearances of Jesus are to the disciples in Galilee. It is an unwelcome reminder to Paul's Gentile converts in the Diaspora that Jesus and his followers are Jews from the Holy Land. And, anyway, Paul is more interested in his own revelatory experiences than he is in those of others. So Paul's converts do not hear much about Galilee, and the tradition of Jesus' appearances there begins to fade.

Moreover, when the disciples proclaim Jesus' resurrection, some people are skeptical. "Did you see the empty tomb?" they ask. At first, the disciples say no, they saw Jesus himself, raised. The skeptics reply, "You saw a ghost, not a resurrected body." Mark's circle, being second generation, is left to say, "The disciples told us they saw Jesus resurrected." A second-hand story of a resurrected crucified criminal is hardly believable. Moreover, by Mark's time, it is clear that Jews are not converting. They expect a militant Messiah, and the first century has many Messiahs more militant than Jesus. Furthermore, Jesus has not returned from heaven, after the pattern of a heavenly Messiah, to bring in the end time. The first generation thought he would return from heaven soon because it believed Jesus' resurrection was a sign of the nearness of the end time.

So Mark, or someone around Mark, devises an empty tomb located in Jerusalem because that is where Jesus dies. When the empty tomb becomes part of the story, inevitably skeptics reply that someone must have stolen the body. So, Matthew adds guards who faint as an angel arrives and who later accept bribes to spread a story about the body's having been stolen.

Everyone knows that ghosts do not eat and are not tangible. Thus, questions about ghosts are answered in details about how and why the disciples touch the body and in scenes of Jesus' eating. Everyone believes in angels and demons and cosmic signs and knows that such things always appear at the death of the famous. Surely they would happen at the resurrection of a man once dead! Embellishing the story with such details not only seems harmless, it seems appropriate.

As soon as stories of disciples visiting an empty tomb circulate, it becomes clear that they must have stayed in Jerusalem. The disciples must have stayed in a house there, and tradition tells of their fear. It is reasonable, then, that they lock the doors. Jesus appears to them behind locked doors. According to John's narrative Jesus has already ascended by this time, so his body need not be flesh and blood, which would not have gone through walls. Luke is the only author who has structured his narrative so he has a resuscitated corpse on his hands rather than a glorified body.

Luke is also the only author of a canonical Gospel to tell of Jesus' ascension. His need for one is clear. A resuscitated corpse is tangible. It cannot appear and vanish at will, and it needs food and shelter. Lots of people will see it, and those in the small town of Bethany, where Jesus often stayed, will recognize it. Luke needs to get rid of the body.

Familiar with the tradition of Elijah's bodily ascension into heaven (2 Kings 2:11), he sends Jesus' body to heaven. In Luke's cosmos, this is perfectly sensible. For Luke, heaven is a place above the azure dome of the sky, literally and physically. But for space-age readers to take Jesus' ascension literally is to confront the bizarre. Perhaps his resuscitated body rocketed to the moon, or Mars, or Andromeda, or.... If it did any of these things, of course, lacking a space suit, it died again—unless it was snatched up by a passing UFO, which is what some people today believe, although not the Jesus scholars.

The thoughtful reader will do well to listen to Paul. His experience of the resurrected Jesus is vivid to him. It changes his life. It does not require belief in an empty tomb and a resuscitated corpse. Peter and James, the brother of Jesus, and the other disciples probably had similar experiences. People have them today. Their lives are changed, too.

Some who read of the authors of the Gospels adding stories of empty tombs, earthquakes, and angelic visitations, and changing the venue of Jesus' appearances from Galilee to

Jerusalem, may conclude that the authors have been dishonest. This is not the case. The first century lacks tape recorders, paper, and books. Historians living in the first century have little written evidence to rely on, even about famous people from literate layers of the culture.

Yet they want to make their histories interesting as well as accurate. They do not have copies of speeches, written or recorded, so they make up speeches someone might have said on an auspicious occasion. And they know that cosmic signs always accompany the births and deaths of heroes, as at the death of Julius Caesar. So they add cosmic signs to their histories, where appropriate. Although the Gospels are not merely histories, the narrative practices of the authors of the Gospels are the accepted practices of first century historians.

The import of Jesus' resurrection

Scholars debate whether Jesus embraces the dream of the end time, but there is no debate about the beliefs of the early followers of the post-resurrection Jesus. They are convinced Jesus is returning soon and will usher in a new age. Paul thinks he will see the return. He tells his converts they will see it before they die. Hence his concern when the Thessalonians and Corinthians worry about the deaths of believers in their midst (1 Thess 4:13; 1 Cor 15:35).

Paul and the others believe Jesus is returning soon because Jesus has been resurrected. The resurrection of the dead is one of the signs of the end time, the beginning of the reconstitution of the twelve tribes of Israel, the commencement of the restoration of the Jews. Jesus is the "first fruits" (1 Cor 15:20). The harvest is imminent.

They already know the outline of events. Either a heavenly Messiah like the son of man foretold in Daniel 7:13-14, or an earthly Messiah like David, will come with righteous men and angels to establish the empire of God and overthrow the powers of this world, the Jewish wicked, and the hated empire of Rome. The followers of Jesus are now able to resolve the ambiguity inherent in the two different Messiah traditions. Jesus, a man of Davidic ancestry, has already come. He is crucified because both the Roman empire and the Jewish powers fear him, the true Emperor. Soon, he will return as the heavenly Messiah and establish God's empire. One man, Jesus, is both the earthly Messiah and the heavenly Messiah.

Very early in the tradition, he also takes on the role of the priestly Messiah who appears in the Essene literature, becoming both the priest who offers the perfect sacrifice and the victim who is the perfect sacrifice. Chapter 9 discusses the concept of Jesus as sacrifice.

The first generation begins to die, and Jesus has not descended with angelic armies. As the hope of his return begins to fade, the Romans destroy the Temple and wreak havoc in Jerusalem. Just such destruction is foretold in the dream of the end time. The earthly Temple will be destroyed, to be replaced by a heavenly one, and the earthly Jerusalem will be exchanged for a heavenly city. One Jewish way of framing this belief is to say that the earthly Jerusalem and Temple are copies of the true Temple and Jerusalem already existing in heaven. At the end time, the earthly is to be destroyed so the heavenly can replace it. Such is the dream in the Epistle to the Hebrews (9:25-28).

Calling on tradition, Mark uses the destruction of the Temple in his Gospel as a second sign of the nearness of the end time. He answers the question of why Jesus' return is delayed by portraying the disciples as stupid and unfaithful, not worthy to see the new age. Mark's converts are different, he implies. They are worthy. This generation will not pass away until Jesus comes. Stay awake and watch (Mark 13:30-37)!

Hope is pregnant once more. A new generation looks eagerly and expectantly for Jesus' cosmic return. Meanwhile, memories of the historical Jesus fade. A few collections of sayings and deeds circulate in written form, hand copied and expensive because the very materials carrying them are scarce. Mark composes his Gospel, recounting some of Jesus' deeds and constructing the first complete passion narrative, and it makes the same slow rounds. Most attention focuses on anticipation of the end time, enacted liturgically in the celebration of the Eucharist. Making converts, in-fighting, and painful separation from the synagogues consume energies. Inspired by the dream of the end time, Christians' central hopes after the resurrection obscure Jesus' original message. Unless, of course, his message is that the end time is imminent. If the imminence of the end time is Jesus' central message, twenty long centuries have proved him wrong.

This part has presented sayings and deeds recorded in the Gospels that scholars think go back to Jesus. It has explored beliefs about Jesus' resurrection. The next part interprets some of these sayings and events.

INTERPRETATIONS

The last part presented historical information about Jesus as accurately as possible in its brief reconstruction of the immense and nuanced scholarship on Jesus. This part interprets this information. It helps us understand where Christianity goes wrong.

Chapter 6 discusses the major division among Jesus scholars that colors every interpretation of Jesus' life. One group interprets Jesus as a prophet whose central focus is the imminent fulfillment of the dream of the end time. The other group sees him as a reformer whose primary concern is this world. The chapter concludes with my own unique interpretation of Jesus as using elements from the dream of the end time to mock it, while living a way of life very different from that envisioned by the dream. Thinking Jesus believes in the dream of the end time is one place Christianity goes wrong.

Chapter 7 is another original contribution to Jesus scholarship. It asks what Jesus considers sin and concludes that he thinks the blindness and hatred of others bred of arrogance, which is rending the fabric of Judaism, is a far worse sin than the actions condemned in the Ten Commandments.

Chapter 8 returns to the resurrection of Jesus to show, in some detail, how belief in it impacts Mark's passion narrative and Paul's understanding of Jesus.

Chapter 9 looks at the cause and meaning of Jesus' death. In particular, it examines the common Christian interpretation of

Jesus' death as a sacrifice, describes how it arose, and inquires whether it is coherent with the historical Jesus' words and deeds. If Jesus thinks sacrifice for sin unnecesssary, Christianity has been arrogant to contradict him. This is another place where Christianity has gone wrong.

Chapter 10 recapitulates the argument briefly.

6 *Prophet or Reformer*

The problem

Scholars in all interpretative camps have sought short, memorable phrases with which to capture the essential Jesus. No one has succeeded, for Jesus is a complex human being. Instead of characterizing Jesus, the title of this chapter characterizes the most important division among Jesus scholars—and not merely contemporary ones. This disagreement dates back to the first searches for the historical Jesus more than a century ago.

Everyone agrees that Jesus is a man filled with God, a charismatic "spirit person" to use Marcus Borg's term for mystic. They also concur on his social class, calling him a "Mediterranean peasant" and "a marginal Jew," to use phrases by John Dominic Crossan and John Meier, respectively. Moreover, they agree that he is a miracle worker, a healer and exorcist, a "doer of wonderful works," to quote Josephus. All also see Jesus as a prophet after the pattern of prophets in the Hebrew Scriptures, that is, a reformer with an eye on the future, like all reformers.

Furthermore, they agree that he is concerned with the empire of God, an empire both present and yet to come. Finally, almost everyone agrees that Jesus is not an armed revolutionary. They think that, if Jesus expects God's empire in the immediate future, he believes God will be the one to usher it in, not human beings, and especially not human beings willing to shed blood for the cause.

This survey of scholarly harmony suggests that consensus exists on the deep issues, disagreement only on details. This is largely true. Yet one issue divides Jesus scholars so fundamentally that it influences their respective interpretations of almost everything else about him. They disagree about Jesus' guiding vision.

One group considers Jesus a reformer focused on how to live in this world, always aware of God's presence here and now and not especially concerned with the dream of the end time, however that may be characterized. The other group deems him a prophet, primarily centered on the dream of the end time, the imminent arrival of a new age when God will restore Israel to greatness, however that dream may be described in detail. Both perspectives have weighty evidence supporting them, which is why the dispute remains unresolved.

Jesus as prophet

The view of Jesus as a prophet of the dream of the end time attracts some of the best Jesus scholars because the evidence for it is clear and well attested. Few Jesus scholars doubt the six pillars on which it rests (although some who characterize Jesus as a reformer hedge sometimes).

(1) Jesus calls twelve disciples. Each Gospel characterizes the disciples by the number twelve throughout, so this number occurs in more than one Gospel source. Moreover, Paul refers to the disciples as twelve even when there were only eleven due to the defection of Judas. This makes "twelve" more than just a number. It has symbolic meaning.

Its symbolic meaning is evident. Twelve is the number of the original tribes of Israel. In the dream of the end time, the dead will be resurrected and the twelve tribes restored. In calling twelve. Jesus is symbolically referring to Israel's original tribes and evoking the dream of the end time. Most scholars in the prophet group think Jesus is calling for the restoration of the Jews, anticipating it, and acting in such a manner that God will make it come about. In this, he would be typical of many first century Jewish Messiahs.

The main evidence counting against Jesus having called twelve is that neither Paul nor the Gospels seems to know who the twelve are. Of the disciples, only Peter, James, and John seem to have become leaders in the movement after the death of Jesus. Most others are not even mentioned as members. Moreover two outstanding leaders of the early assemblies are not from the original twelve, namely Paul and James, the brother of Jesus, head of the assembly in Jerusalem. Jesus begins with a rather mundane inner circle, and most never acquire enough reputation to be remembered, for good or ill.

(2) Jesus causes an incident in the Temple. He chases out buyers and sellers, overturns furniture, and tries to stop people from walking through the Temple. This series of incidents is one of the most difficult in the Gospels to interpret. Most scholars in both camps are sure it happens. Most are certain Jesus intends it to be symbolic, for two reasons. First, prophets in the Hebrew Scriptures carry out symbolic acts in the Temple, so there is precedent for symbolic, prophetic behavior there. Second, had it been a realistic attempt to stop the operation of the Temple, Jesus would have been arrested or, more likely, killed by the authorities on the spot. Not only are the Temple precincts sacred, but this is Passover, with huge crowds entering the city to celebrate the great feast of Jewish liberation. Never likely to be lenient, the authorities are especially nervous of crowds in their own occupied country celebrating their ancestors' liberation.

Those in the prophet group think Jesus predicts the destruction of the Temple. They have a particularly strong case because the prediction in the Gospels that not one stone will be left upon another turns out to be false. The Romans burn the Temple, and parts of the western wall stand to this day, stone on stone. Yet the Gospels are written after 70, so their authors know what actually happens. If they invent the prediction, why do they invent a false one?

The prophet group also thinks Jesus enacts the destruction of the Temple symbolically by overturning furniture. Its destruction is one of the signs of the end time. Symbolically, Jesus is saying the end time is near.

(3) Jesus speaks often of God's empire. Both groups agree on this point, and both agree that the empire is both present and still to come. Their disagreement involves differences of emphasis.

(4) The Romans crucify Jesus. This is one of the absolutely certain historical events. All agree.

(5) The most plausible reason for the Romans to crucify Jesus is because they think Jesus sees himself and/or is seen by others as a ruler, an emperor. Again, almost everyone agrees that this is what the Romans think. Many also hold that a plaque saying something like "Emperor of the Jews" accompanies Jesus to his death. Romans commonly place plaques inscribed with criminals' crimes around their necks, and more than one Gospel source reports that such a plaque accompanies Jesus. The interpretative question is whether the Roman understanding of Jesus' behavior is correct. The prophet group depicts Jesus as calling himself emperor, at least among his inner circle, and expecting God's rule to come immediately. In God's empire, Jesus will be emperor or viceroy, and the twelve disciples judges and/or rulers of the restored twelve tribes. (The judges of the twelve tribes before the advent of emperors were both judges and rulers.)

(6) Jesus is a disciple of John the Baptist who is a preacher of the imminent end time, and the early assemblies expect the end at any moment. It is difficult to imagine Jesus living temporally between these two groups while ignoring the end time dream.

This is the case for interpreting Jesus as a prophet of the end time. It is strong. But so is the case of the group that perceives Jesus as a reformer.

Jesus as reformer

The reformers have two intertwined arguments, both backed by strong evidence. First, Jesus lives and preaches an alternative lifestyle and, so, is concerned with how to live here and now. Second, the content of his life and preaching does not fit the dream of the end time. Here is the reformers' evidence.

(1) When Jesus speaks of the empire of God, his most common images of it are of something small, hidden and precious, present and available now. His deeds are bringing it about now. He cures the sick, exorcises the possessed, and apparently raises the dead. God is bringing the empire in through him, now, in this life.

(2) In both his works and his words, Jesus is inclusive in a world of exclusivity. He tears down the boundaries established by his society when he eats with the outcast and wicked, heals lepers, ignores the purity codes, speaks to women in public, and welcomes women followers. Jesus' inclusiveness suggests that he would not welcome the world of the end time dream from which so many are excluded.

(3) Jesus is egalitarian in a world of hierarchies. He treats women, the poor, and the outcast as worthwhile, asks the rich to give up their riches, and the high to step down. The dream of the end time is not egalitarian. It envisions the restoration of a hierarchical society.

(4) The Temple incident is a protest against exploitation by the Temple system, which is why he chases out the buyers and sellers. While the Temple authorities proclaim the necessity of Temple sacrifices for the forgiveness of sins, Jesus forgives sins outside the Temple system, without the necessity of sacrifices. To Jesus the spirit person, God is close and

compassionate. Worshiping God does not requiring priestly mediators. A restored Temple at the end of time is hardly central to Jesus' vision.

(5) Jesus rejects kinship ties, declaring his followers his family. His twelve disciples are not heads of kinship clans. Jesus is not interested in the restoration of kinship implied by the renewal of the tribes, each of which is a kinship clan.

(6) Jesus adopts the life-style of an itinerant preacher and speaks against wealth. He is not concerned with possessions of any sort, in contrast to the end time dream, which is deeply committed to the restoration of the land to the Jews.

(7) Jesus' compassion and his own forgiveness of sins speak against his belief in the dream of the end time, with its terrible war that destroys the wicked and rescues the righteous.

These, too, are good arguments. And, so, presently there is an impasse on a fundamental issue in Jesus scholarship. I think a resolution is possible. Here it is.

Resolving the problem

The people whom Jews consider righteous in Jesus' day are the Pharisees, the Essenes, and James, the brother of Jesus, a man known as "James the Righteous" for his strict keeping of rules of fasting, ritual bathing, and kosher. The reason these righteous Jews follow the religious and moral laws so strictly is to keep God in their presence, whether in the Temple, at the table of the Pharisees, or with the company of Essenes. All the factions fear God will leave them unless they keep the rules. This perspective is similar to that of the Romans who think the gods of their enemies will desert their enemies and join the Romans if only the Romans display greater piety toward the gods than their enemies do. Piety keeps the gods and/or God present.

When John the Baptist appears in the Gospels, he has the mission statement of the Essenes on his lips and preaches their message of the imminent end time, but he has ceased practicing their life of daily ritual, if he once did. Moreover, he preaches that repentance is required for salvation and initiates a new rite, baptism, to symbolize it. Jesus becomes his disciple and accepts his baptism.

At his baptism, Jesus has a powerful religious experience, presented in Mark 1:9-11, where the heavens open, the Spirit descends, and a voice says, "'You are my Son, the beloved; with you I am well pleased.'" Most scholars doubt the historicity of the details, which are clearly dramatized and symbolic. Yet something happens, something so powerful that Jesus disappears into the desert and remains there alone for many days.

Apparently, the accounts retain a central historical truth. Jesus' experience of God is of God's pervasive presence, God's loving intimacy, and God's acceptance of him. The voice does not say, "Your repentance is insufficient," or "Please change," but "I love you, and you have pleased me." It is as if tension and struggle go out of the relationship. Jesus sees that he does not need to do particular things to keep God present or to retain God's approval. God is present and approves.

This is an experience similar to that of other mystics and, today, of people revived by modern medicine after undergoing near-death experiences. After such experiences, people see differently. They are more aware of God's love, compassion, and forgiveness, and they want to serve others and carry the message of God's goodness to them.

So, when Jesus returns from the desert, he does not rejoin John. He has seen differently, and he returns to preach a different message. He still speaks of the empire of God, but it is not the empire envisioned by John or the Essenes in the dream of the end time. Rather, he speaks of a tiny, hidden, but precious empire, worth giving up everything else to acquire, here and now, as Jesus himself has done. Jesus has cut John's message in two. Like John, he preaches the forgiveness of sins and brings forgiveness to those who come to him, without requiring sacrifice.

But he rejects the other half of the message, the sudden advent of God in wrath to establish an empire of the repentant at the end of time. Moreover, he rejects the whole idea of it as an empire similar in many respects to that of Rome around him, just as he rejects the idea of resurrected life as similar to the lives around him.

Jesus not only proclaims a different empire, he mocks specific, familiar elements of the empire of the end time.

The depth of the chasm that separates Jesus' thought from the dream of the end time appears in his preaching. When he contrasts the righteous person with the sinner, he reverses the dream's stereotypes, condemning the righteous Pharisee and condoning the sinful tax collector. This parable is so important for understanding Jesus that it is discussed at length in the following chapter.

When Jesus confronts those who accuse a woman of adultery, he insists they acknowledge their own sins before condemning her. In a well-attested saying, he asks us to take the log out of our own eyes before we try to remove the speck from the eyes of others (Matt 7:3-5). Rather than hating our enemies, Jesus asks us to love them. Many of Jesus' stories and sayings mock the dream of the end time, whose fiery judgment separates people into two groups, vindicates the righteous, and condemns the unrighteous to everlasting death or torment.

The Jews of Jesus' day think a person's sins cause sickness, possession, and death, and that health and wealth are God's reward for righteousness. Jesus' healings, exorcisms, apparent resuscitations, and inclusiveness toward the poor and outcast symbolize God's forgiveness, here and now, and God's preference for the poor. They are an insult to the Essenes and the Temple, both of whom exclude the blind, lame, crippled, women, and children from their inner precincts. Jesus' consorting with the poor and sinners mocks the dream of the end time with its emphasis on righteousness, maintenance of hierarchies, and eternally dead or tormented sinners.

Jesus lives as an itinerant, rejecting possessions and kinship ties. The end time dream is of the restoration of land to its rightful owners and the reconstitution of kinship clans. Jesus' life mocks the dream.

Jesus calls twelve disciples in order to announce that God's empire is already here. Mark portrays the disciples as twelve disreputable men, weak in understanding and unfaithful in deed. Matthew and Luke are kinder, but all say that most are fishermen and one a tax collector—hardly righteous men by the standards of the Sadducees, the Essenes, the Pharisees, or the dream of the end time. In choosing such ordinary men, Jesus shows that God's empire comes to the lowly, is found in daily life here and now, and does not need to wait for the arrival of archetypally righteous men such as the Davidic Messiah and the judges in the dream of the end time.

In calling twelve, Jesus may also be mocking the governing council of the Essenes, which is composed of twelve, too.

Especially insulting to the dream is Jesus' banqueting with his followers while others fast and pray, riot and die, for its fulfillment. In the eyes of the ascetic righteous, Jesus appears to be a glutton and a drunkard. Jesus sees differently. He is celebrating the presence of God here and now, God's love of humanity, and God's fatherly care and intimacy.

People previously near to Jesus realize his acts and words mock the dream. This is at least partly why his hometown rejects him, his family thinks him crazy, and the Jewish authorities have him killed. His mockery of the dream makes many Jews angry, no matter what their faction, for the dream of the end time in one guise or another heralds the liberation, purification, and restoration of Israel that almost every Jew desires.

If Jesus rides into Jerusalem on a donkey, he does so in mockery of the Davidic hero and coming Messiah who will raise a mighty army of the righteous to liberate the land. Men on donkeys are unlikely to defeat Roman legions. Moreover, Jesus tells the

Jews to love their enemies rather than to drive them out of the Holy Land.

Jesus makes symbolic gestures against the Temple in the Temple and predicts the destruction of the Temple. Most scholars agree that these events and sayings are historical, but they disagree about their meaning.

The prediction of the destruction of the Temple seems especially likely to be historical. It displays the exaggeration so typical of Jesus when he says, "'Not one stone will be left here upon another; all will be thrown down'" (Mark 13:2). The Temple encompasses some thirty-five acres, with stones weighing tons. Moreover, the Gospel authors write after the destruction of the Temple, so they know fire destroys it. The western wall still stands, stone on stone. Jesus' prediction must have been so widely known that the Gospel writers were reluctant to change it to fit the facts.

Jesus' prediction of the destruction of the Temple highlights his concern about murderous factionalism among the Jews. We know the final Jewish civil war starts at the Temple. Jesus can see it coming, and he is not the only one. His prediction warns the militants to embrace peace, or the Romans will destroy the Jews, if the Jews do not destroy themselves first. Jesus makes his entreaty for peace because he knows the cosmic holy war dreamed of by the militants will never come. God's empire is already here. Jesus' plea for peace also accords with what scholars in both camps already agree is Jesus stance against violence.

His actions against the Temple are more difficult to interpret. The Temple is not only huge, but also crowded. Only the people near him would have been aware of his gestures. He could not have stopped the traffic through the Temple. If he had seriously tried, or if he had overturned much furniture, the authorities would most likely have killed him then and there.

At least one scholar has suggested that, if Jesus wanted to symbolize the destruction of the Temple, he could have broken a clay jar as Jeremiah did (Jere 19:1, 10-11). But Jeremiah was not in the Temple. He was in the Hinnom Valley protesting idolatry and predicting the destruction of Israel by foreign nations. His prophecy does not fit Jesus' situation. Moreover, it might have been misunderstood as a protest against the Roman occupation. To make such a protest would have been dangerous. Furthermore, Jesus is not interested in making such a protest. He teaches inclusion and love of enemies instead of rebellion.

Jesus' gestures seem designed to indicate the end of the Temple's functioning. However, whether they mean the end of Passover celebrations or the end of sacrifices in general is unclear. They could mean much less. They might have been simply gestures of frustration, a cry of "Stop! Listen to me!"

The crowded Temple, with people pushing and shoving, buying and selling, might have been for Jesus like Wal-Mart on Christmas Eve is for those who deplore the commercialization of Christmas. His chasing out the buyers and sellers and trying to stop the Temple traffic might have meant, "Everyone is so busy with the details and requirements of the festival that no one stops to listen for God, who is here among us, right now." This interpretation harmonizes with Jesus' message in Galilee, his impatience with details and requirements, his condemnation of public piety, and his own practice of going off alone to pray, where he, like Elijah (1 Kings 19:11-18), can hear God speaking out of the silence. Jesus could have been doing many things other than symbolizing the destruction of the Temple at the imminent end of time.

Jesus' mockery of the Jewish dream of the end time, his disturbance in the Temple, his speaking publicly of the empire of God, explain Jesus' arrest and crucifixion. His mockery of the dream angers Jews of almost every faction, not merely the Temple administrators. His warning of the destruction of the Temple and his disturbance of its business both anger and frighten the Temple authorities, whose livelihood rests on the continuance of Temple business and whose security lies in keeping the Roman peace in Jerusalem. And whatever his fellow Jews understand of his mockery of their dream, the Romans see a man pretending to be emperor of the Jews who is disturbing the peace. They tolerate neither, especially during Passover.

Jesus' mockery of the dream of the end time leads to his crucifixion. He dies as a protest against the dream that drives so much Jewish factionalism and fratricide. He leaves this life as a witness that God's empire is present and available now.

Not everyone sees God's empire present here and now. Some who do see it call it evil. According to Jesus, sin blinds them both. This sin is not in the Ten Commandments. It is intimately related to the dream of the end time.

7 | *Sin*

The parables

The Gospels say very little about what constitutes sin. A glance down the relevant entries in *Roget's Thesaurus of the Bible* or a concordance shows the citations leaping from the Hebrew Scriptures to Paul's letters, skipping the Gospels almost entirely. Jesus' parables are largely about the empire of God. Jesus forgives sins without discussing sin. Because his listeners are Jews like himself, perhaps what is sinful is too obvious for reflection.

Nor do Jesus scholars say much about what Jesus considers sinful. Therefore, this chapter depends largely on my own scholarship and the scholarship of the Jesus Seminar. I have limited the Gospel passages discussed in this chapter to those the Jesus Seminar thinks go back to Jesus, for the Seminar alone has published a detailed account of which sayings are his (Funk and the Jesus Seminar 1993).

The parable the Seminar believes Jesus tells that touches most nearly on sin is that of the Pharisee and the tax collector. Here it is, still from the NRSV.

> Two men went up to the temple to pray, one a Pharisee and the other a tax collector. The Pharisee, standing by himself, was praying thus, "God, I thank you that I am

> not like other people: thieves, rogues, adulterers, or even like this tax collector. I fast twice a week; I give a tenth of all my income." But the tax collector, standing far off, would not even look up to heaven, but was beating his breast and saying, "God, be merciful to me, a sinner!" I tell you, this man went down to his home justified rather than the other. (Luke 18:10-14a)

Jesus contrasts two stereotypical Jewish figures, the Pharisee, an admired lay religious leader, and the tax collector, a despised traitor and thief.

Some of the Greek is difficult to translate. The word rendered "thieves" is very negative. It means filled with greed, rapacious, an extortionist, a swindler. The word translated as "rogues" means unrighteous, one who breaks the law (Torah).

In the parable, the Pharisee is recognizably a good man. He is faithful to his wife, honest, and charitable. His religious works exceed the demands of the law.

The tax collector is recognizably despicable. Jewish tax collectors are local notables who collaborate with Rome to squeeze taxes out of their own kindred. They contract with their region to collect a specified amount of money for Rome. If they collect more than the contract stipulates, they keep it. The temptations of the position must have been overwhelming, turning once honest people into extortionists who break the eighth commandment, that against stealing (Exod 20:15) and perhaps the ninth, that against bearing false witness (Exod 20:16).

Yet Jesus condemns the Pharisee. The Gospels usually charge the Pharisees with hypocrisy, but this parable contains no hint that the Pharisee is a hypocrite. He has kept the law (Torah). This is why he is thankful. His thankfulness for being unlike others is not unusual. It lies deep in the Jewish prayer tradition.

The Pharisee appears to think he is sinless if he has followed the law. This is not unusual, either. Paul, who was reared as a Pharisee, thinks the same about himself. "As to the law, a Pharisee;

. . . as to righteousness under the law, blameless" (Phil 3:5b-6). Paul never applies the term common in biblical and rabbinic writings for repentance and a return to righteousness to himself. He does not feel the need to return to righteousness, for he had not been unrighteous (Segal 1990, 20). Nonetheless, Paul the convert is aware of his weakness and sinfulness, as the Pharisee in Jesus' story never is.

The Pharisee could have prayed differently. The subject of his prayer might have been "God" instead of "I." A humbler, more self-aware man might have thanked God for helping him resist the temptations of greed and lust that haunt human life. He might have thanked God for being so wealthy he can afford to be charitable and to fast, voluntary fasting being a luxury reserved for those who have enough to eat. He might have thanked God he was not engaged in such a tempting and despised livelihood as tax collecting. He might have seen how much like other people he is, not how different (and superior!). He might have pitied the tax collector.

He could be the very man whom Jesus asks, "'Why do you see the speck in your neighbor's eye, but do not notice the log in your own eye?'" (Luke 7:3). The parable and the saying condemn ignorance of one's own sinfulness, a kind of blindness about the lusts of the self. They condemn arrogance that denigrates others. This is precisely the self-ignorance, arrogance, and hatred of others that consumes so much of the lives of the dreamers of the end time dream.

Luke's Jesus not only condemns the Pharisee, he calls the tax collector "justified." The Greek word translated as "justified" means the establishment of a person as just, free of guilt, righteous. The tax collector does only two things. He confesses his own sinfulness, and he asks God for mercy. Because Jesus pronounces him justified, Jesus must think these actions are sufficient for righteousness.

Luke's Prodigal Son does even less than the tax collector. He does not ask for mercy, that is, restoration, but plans to ask his father to treat him as a hired hand. Yet he clearly admits his guilt: "'Father, I have sinned against heaven and before you. I am no longer worthy to be called your son'" (Luke 15:21). The father (God) cuts him short. Before the son can ask for a position as a hired hand, the father calls for a robe, a ring, sandals, and the fatted calf, and celebrates his son's return. Admitting one's sinfulness is apparently sufficient to warrant forgiveness. Admitting one's sinfulness requires self-knowledge. It requires seeing oneself as a human being similar to others.

The Prodigal Son has an elder brother. When he hears the celebration and discovers its cause, he angrily resents it. His father replies, "'Son, you are always with me, and all that is mine is yours. But we had to celebrate and rejoice because this brother of yours was dead and has come to life; he was lost and has been found'" (15:31-32). The father offers an adequate explanation of his own behavior. He does not condemn his eldest son, who, in turn, had not condemned his brother. Yet the elder brother is certainly aware of the contrast between his own righteousness and his brother's sin. In this, he resembles the righteous of the Jewish factions. The elder brother receives something more like justice than mercy, and he is not pleased.

Matthew 20:1-15 tells an unrelated parable from a different source with a similar twist. This is the story of the laborers, some of whom a landowner (God) hires in the morning and promises a certain wage, and some of whom he hires later in the day. When pay time comes, the landowner pays the early workers the wage he had promised. He pays the later ones an equal amount. Those who worked all day grumble that those hired later hardly worked at all, yet they have been paid a full day's wage. The landowner replies that he has been just, for he has paid the wage he promised. Those hired early should not envy the landowner's generosity to others.

Both parables are about God's empire, Matthew's explicitly so. God's generosity to sinners angers the righteous when they see it. In other parables of the empire of God, Jesus has implied that some perceive God's empire, yet call it evil. This happens here, too. Everywhere, God's empire overturns society's expectations. Those desiring justice see God's mercy as too generous and compassionate. Some who long for justice, that is, the sword of God raised against Rome, must see God as too generous, too. They are impatient for the fulfillment of the dream of the end time, for the vindication of themselves as righteous and the condemnation of sinners beneath God's wrath. They are angry with the God whom Matthew's Jesus says "'makes his sun rise on the evil and on the good, and sends his rain on the righteous and the unrighteous'" (Matt 5:45).

And, yet, the characters in the parables seem to get what they have most desired. Those laboring obediently who consider themselves justified and therefore seek justice receive justice. Those who see their own sin and therefore desire mercy obtain mercy. The Pharisee who is so ready to censure the tax collector apparently receives what he finds most attractive, condemnation. The reader suspects he would have been even more angry and censorious than the elder brother and the early laborers had he known of Jesus' justification of the tax collector.

Jesus' central thesis about sin seems to be that blindness to one's own sin leads to arrogance and the condemnation of others. The arrogant plead for justice and vindication for themselves and cry for the condemnation of others. One of the main themes of the dream of the end time, of course, is the vindication of the righteous and the condemnation of the wicked.

When Jesus teaches about sin, he implies that this dream is a hallucination of the blind. The righteous have eyes filled with logs. They are angry when God's mercy equalizes people, bringing the same wages to all and gathering all together in one joyous banquet for the lost and found sinner. Were their eyes open, they would understand that they, too, are forgiven and invited to be guests at God's banquet. Instead, they reject the invitation (Luke 14:16-24). Such righteous people devise and sustain factions. They kindle and enflame fratricidal hatred everywhere.

Thus, Jesus' insight about sin is not limited to Judaism or even to religion. It is an insight about human nature. Give any group of people an arbitrary set of rules, then have one group be obedient, the other disobedient. Very quickly, the obedient will think themselves better than the disobedient and pronounce themselves righteous. If everyone involved thinks the rules come from God, a highly volatile situation will develop. It will become inflammatory if several conflicting sets of rules are involved, each the prized code of a different group. This is the situation in the Holy Land before and during Jesus' lifetime. He sees the danger. He is not objecting to the content of the rules as such, but to a way of life based on rules that inevitably lead to self-righteousness, hatred, and conflict.

Jesus implies that God will judge people by the standards by which they judge others. This is common wisdom in Judaism, a reminder of Jesus' deep immersion in Jewish traditions. If God judges people by their own standards, those who break the law, admit it, and long for mercy are better off than those who keep the law, count themselves justified, and demand justice. Many passages in the Gospels express a similar outlook. There is humor here, or irony, justice and generosity wonderfully combined. It is a just-and-merciful God who judges people by the judgment they apply, thus granting them their hearts' deepest desires. In Jesus's vision God's judgment does not favor the dreamers of the end time dream.

The shorter sayings

"'There is nothing outside a person that by going in can defile, but the things that come out are what defile'" (Mark 7:15). This saying confronts the laws of purity and pollution that constitute so much of the Judaism of the two first centuries. Those laws say that what goes in defiles, that certain foods are unholy. The Jews have other rules of purity and pollution, laws covering ejaculation, menstruation, cooking, cleaning, bathing, bearing babies, and burying the dead. To follow the rules is to live righteously.

Jesus scholars disagree about whether Jesus thinks people should ignore the purity laws. Perhaps this is because ignoring particular laws is not the problem Jesus addresses. He thinks a life so concerned with lawful righteousness breeds exclusion and hatred and blinds people to their common sinfulness and humanity. Jesus is a religious reformer concerned with the development of the human personality under a religion of laws. He thinks legalistic personalities thrive on hatred and factionalism.

Jesus' question, "'Are grapes gathered from thorns, or figs from thistles?'" (Matt 7:16b) supports this view. It shows that the things coming out of a person reflect that person's personality, spirit, or character. As grapevines produce grapes and fig trees, figs, so from their good or evil characters, people produce good or evil deeds.

"'It is easier for a camel to go through the eye of a needle than for someone who is rich to enter the kingdom of God'" (Mark 10:25). "'Blessed are you who are poor, for yours is the kingdom of God. Blessed are you who are hungry now, for you will be filled. Blessed are you who weep now, for you will laugh'" (Luke 6:20-21).

Jesus lives in an unjust society. The rich have become wealthy by exploiting the poor, and they have acquired the spoils of war, including slaves. In order to eat, pay taxes, or support their families, the poor sometimes sell their children into slavery. Jesus' anger at the rich is not anger at riches, but at callousness, the unjust distribution of property and the exploitation that leave the poor destitute.

Moreover, the rich believe they merit their wealth while the poor deserve their poverty. Jesus sees more clearly. He sees that the rich of his day get rich by exploitation and that the poor of his day can never overcome their poverty no matter how hard they work. He sees the blindness of the rich as he sees that of the

Pharisee. Both deny their own sinfulness. The rich ignore the sinful structures of their society as well. Worse, they support them and crucify those who rebel.

In contrast, the poor are much more likely to acknowledge their sinfulness and, so, to enter God's empire, for they are less observant of the laws of purity and pollution. They are downtrodden and accused of wickedness. Those who break the Ten Commandments and other Torah laws, whether poor or not, are also likely to enter, for they know they are sinful and deeply in need of God's mercy.

Jesus is well within Jewish tradition when he emphasizes human sinfulness and need for mercy while minimizing Torah law. Genesis pronounces human beings sinful before the flood (Gen 6:5; 6:12) and after (Gen 8:21). Kings and Chronicles say everyone sins (1 Kings 8:46; 2 Chron 6:36). The Psalms repeatedly proclaim the sinfulness of all people, even the righteous (Pss. 14:3; 53:3; 143:2; 40:12; 130:3). The prophets say God desires mercy, not sacrifice (Hos 6:6) and detests religious festivals, songs, and sacrifices (Isa 1: 11-14; Amos 5:21-23). Jesus is a decidedly Jewish religious reformer. He applies ancient scriptural ideas about sin to his own social context.

The social context

Hebrew, Egyptian, Greek, and Roman literature all represent Jews as exclusive. The ancient world accuses Jews of impiety because they will not worship the gods and because their God is exclusive. It accuses them of misanthropy because they reject religious art that represents the gods in human form, consider themselves superior as God's chosen people, and mutilate the human body by circumcision (Schafer 1997). Exclusion is their way of life. Purity and pollution laws accentuate and reinforce their exclusiveness.

The Jewish emphasis on exclusiveness produces factionalism within Jewish culture. Jewish factionalism has a long history, going back at least to the establishment of the Second Temple. When the exiles return from Babylon and begin rebuilding the Temple in about 520 BCE, the book of Ezra reports that people who have long occupied the land say, "'Let us build with you, for we worship your God as you do, and we have been sacrificing to him ever since the days of King Esar-haddon of Assyria who brought us here'" (4:2), but the returned exiles refuse (4:3). When Ezra himself arrives in 458 BCE, he commands the returned exiles who had married the women of the land to separate themselves from their wives and children (Ezra 9 and 10).

After the Maccabbeans achieve Jewish independence in 141 BCE, civil wars break out among the Jews. According to Josephus (*War* IV.6), the ruler Alexander Jannaeus crucifies eight hundred Pharisees. Later, Salome Alexandra sides with the Pharisees, deprives the Sadducees of office and exiles the Essenes. After the Romans restore peace in 63 BCE, Sicarii and Zealots assassinate Jews who collaborate with Rome. Jewish factionalism is murderous. It is far more dangerous to Jewish society than individuals who break the Ten Commandments.

Each faction establishes its own calendars, purity rules, leaders, and even temples. In their factionalism, the Jews are unlike the Romans whose gods are inclusive, whose sociality is legendary, and whose citizens come from many cities, nations, and ethnic groups.

Jesus knows all this. He grows up in Nazareth, only four miles from the Roman city of Sepphoris, and launches his mission from Capernaum, up the seacoast from the Roman city of Tiberius. He travels in the Decapolis, a federation of Roman cities. John Dominic Crossan, a Jesus scholar who has studied Jesus' social context carefully, thinks Jesus is deeply influenced by the Romans, especially by a group of traveling philosophers called Cynics. Like Jesus, the Cynics are itinerant preachers who teach through exaggerated aphorisms. Like him, they embrace poverty and simplicity, reject convention, and practice a distinctive way of life. Like him, they claim a common human nature and reject cultural practices that exclude. But they are Roman and urban. Jesus is Jewish and rural. Crossan characterizes Jesus as a "*peasant Jewish Cynic*" (Crossan 1991, 421).

Perhaps the man who asks the Jews to love their enemies and pray for their persecutors visited the Roman cities sufficiently to learn the value of inclusiveness and to see the ugliness of the end time dream. But Jesus was never a Cynic. His words show no sign of the rational philosophical skepticism that arises in Greece and invades Rome. He never engages in philosophical analysis. Instead, he sees a new vision of God's empire and responds like a Jewish prophet. If he learns inclusiveness from Rome, he translates it into Jewish terms. The Hebrew Scriptures speak of humanity's common sinfulness. Jesus is convinced. That is why he condemns the Pharisee, who sees himself as righteous because law-abiding, and also why he seeks baptism from John the Baptist.

Jesus' baptism

Mark's Gospel portrays John the Baptist as "proclaiming a baptism of repentance for the forgiveness of sins" and the people who come to him as "confessing their sins" at their baptism (1:4-5). Luke and Matthew follow Mark. Josephus' account is similar.

> John, that was called the *Baptist* . . . was a good man, and commanded the Jews to exercise virtue, both as to righteousness towards one another, and piety towards God, and so to come to baptism; for that the washing . . . would be acceptable to him, if they made use of it, not in order to the putting away, [or remission] of some sins [only,] but for the purification of the body, supposing still that the soul was thoroughly purified beforehand by righteousness. (*Antiquities* V.2)

Both the synoptic Christian Gospels and the Jewish historian portray John the Baptist as a preacher whose baptism is directly linked to sin and purification.

Jesus requests and receives John's baptism. Surely Jesus knows the purpose of John's baptism. Everyone else does. John's baptism signifies repentance. Those he baptizes confess their sins. Afterwards, they think of themselves as purified. Jesus, too, must have come to John confessing his sins, seeking remission and purification.

This interpretation fits Mark's record at 10:18, which Matthew and Luke retain. Someone addresses Jesus as "'good.'" Jesus replies, "'Why do you call me good? No one is good but God alone.'" The interpretation fits the Jewish tradition that all human beings are sinners. It fits the fact that Jesus is a peasant from Galilee who has no reason to think of himself as righteous, as a Pharisee or an Essene might. It fits Jesus' message that all are sinful, and it fits his sense that God is merciful to those who confess their sins. It also fits his message of inclusiveness.

If Jesus does not consider himself sinful, he is an appalling hypocrite.

Jesus considers himself sinful, so at his baptism he confesses, trusting God's mercy and compassion. The result is a profound deepening of his relationship with God, symbolized in the Gospels by the descending dove, the voice from heaven, and Jesus' sojourn in the wilderness. His confession deepens his intimacy with God, and that deepened intimacy assures him that God forgives sins.

Returning from the wilderness, Jesus carries that message through Galilee and beyond. God forgives sins outside the Temple system. God forgives those who confess and is merciful to all who ask for mercy. But to those who want their own righteousness vindicated and the wicked condemned, Jesus is not so gentle. He calls them blind, reproves their arrogance and exclusiveness, and mocks their end time dream.

Because Jesus considers himself sinful, he must reject the end time dream. In it, sinners are condemned. Only the righteous are saved. Like John the Baptist, Jesus must believe God saves forgiven sinners.

Jesus adds two things to the little that is known of John the Baptist's message. First, salvation is now, not in a future idealized world. Second, everyone must repent. The righteous must repent along with the sinners. Jesus calls all the righteous to repent, the Pharisee who has kept the law, the elder brother who has obeyed his father, and the early laborers who have worked hard all day for their wage. He asks them to repent their exclusiveness, their lack of compassion and generosity, and their condemnation of others.

The Gospels speak of an unforgivable sin (Matt 12:32b). The Jesus Seminar does not think the idea comes from Jesus. I think the concept goes back to Jesus, but the details have been Christianized. The Pharisee, the elder brother, and the early laborers do not know they are sinful. They think they are righteous. Jesus finds sin here—not in their obedience, but in their sense of superiority, their inability to include themselves among common humanity, their arrogance, their unwillingness to repent. If God requires repentance for forgiveness and renders justice to the righteous, God does not forgive the righteous or treat them with mercy. Even if they are in God's empire, they do not think of themselves as fairly treated there. They are not as well off as those who repent.

Furthermore, Jesus indicates that many of the righteous are not in God's empire at all. They do not like it and, so, reject it. God cannot welcome them in, for they will not come. For Jesus, the unforgivable sin is the arrogance and hatred of others that leads to the murderous factionalism unraveling the many-colored coat of Judaism. It is unforgivable because those ensnared in it do not want forgiveness. Thus, they are further removed from God than sinners who break the Ten Commandments and repent.

If Jesus' followers ever understand his message, they soon forget it. Their knowledge of the historical Jesus is overwhelmed by their belief that God has raised Jesus from the dead. Believing in Jesus' resurrection, they begin to dream once more of the imminent end time. The next two chapters follow their dreams.

8 | *The Resurrection Revisited*

The limitations of history

No student of the historical Jesus will comment as a historian on the historicity of the resurrection of Jesus. The resurrection is not the sort of event that can be treated as historical. There are no historical criteria to apply to a unique event occurring somewhere other than in the material world. However, scholars can compare events, and when they do, they see something like the following.

The frightened disciples desert Jesus at his arrest and flee back to Galilee. There, they resume their old occupations. Presumably, they think Jesus' mission has failed with his death, like the missions of so many first century Messiahs. Sometime thereafter, some of the disciples are in the synagogues and streets announcing that Jesus, whom the Romans crucified, has been raised from the dead. They are no longer frightened. Instead, they risk beatings, ejection from synagogues, and even death, to proclaim Jesus' resurrection.

Something happened. The disciples say they have had an extraordinary experience. After Jesus' crucifixion and death, they encountered him alive again. They interpret their experience as meeting the resurrected Jesus rather than his ghost or spirit. They think Jesus' resurrection vindicates his life, for the dream of the end time says the righteous dead will be vindicated through resurrection. Jesus is the "first fruits," to use Paul's expression. Before Jesus' generation passes away, God will raise all the righteous dead.

The Gospel writers seem to be just as perplexed as the reader about how to distinguish between a ghost or a disembodied spirit and a resurrected human being. Mark evades the issue by avoiding stories of post-resurrection appearances. At the other extreme, Luke wrestles with the embarrassment of a resuscitated corpse. Matthew has one rather magical appearance on top of a mountain with only the disciples present, avoiding Luke's problem of why people other than the disciples fail to see Jesus. John depicts an ascended Jesus returning with a body that can be touched and consume food, yet appears and disappears in a locked room—the best of both worlds, but paradoxical.

In a curious passage in 2 Corinthians 12:2-5, Paul tells of his ecstatic transportation to paradise where he meets the resurrected Jesus. Paul does not know whether he himself is embodied. This makes it extraordinarily difficult to say in what sense Jesus is embodied. In the passages on resurrection in general, Paul speaks of glorified bodies unlike those of flesh and blood. No one can say with certainty what difference exists between a glorified body and a ghostly one, which is often compared to a mist or cloud. Maybe the glorified body is brighter and/or of greater density.

So, using historical material across sources, it is difficult to ascertain with any consistency how to think of resurrected bodies and impossible to deal with Jesus' resurrection as history. Knowing the history of the Jesus movement and other messianic movements, historians note that the Jesus movement expands while others die out. The only (unhistorical) explanation Jesus scholars have for this is that God raised Jesus from the dead. Sociological explanations for the success of the movement are available, but speculative, and not worth pursuing here. Worth pursuing is how belief in the resurrection of Jesus influences the earliest canonical portraits of him.

Mark's portrait

Unlike Paul, Mark is interested in the historical Jesus, especially his sojourn in Jerusalem, which constitutes about one-third of Mark's Gospel. Mark is a Gentile who writes for Gentiles, and he and his sources are unfamiliar with the details of the events in Jerusalem. Because Mark and his sources believe Jesus' words and actions fulfill the Hebrew Scriptures, they search the Greek translation, the Septuagint, to fill in details of Jesus' life unknown to them otherwise. A clear example of this is the scene in Gethsemane, which has many parallels with the narrative about David found in 2 Samuel 15-17 in which David flees in fear of his life across the Kidron valley and up the Mount of Olives, weeping as he goes. He is running from men who have betrayed him, one by means of a kiss. In Mark 14:26-46, Jesus, too, crosses the Kidron valley and climbs the Mount of Olives. Sorrowful, Jesus is betrayed by a kiss.

Many scholars think the details of Jesus' passion, beginning at Mark 15, take their inspiration from the Septuagint. The flogging, striking, and spitting come from Isaiah 50:6, and details of royal investiture similar to the robing of Jesus in purple occur in stories about the earthly Joseph (Gen 41:40-45), a visionary Joseph (Zech 3:1-5), and Mordecai (Esther 6:6-11). Whether Mark's Gentile audience would understand the allusions is unclear. The book of Esther, the only book in the current Jewish canon not found even in fragments among the Dead Sea Scrolls, may have been obscure even to Jews.

But Mark's readers know Roman practices from their own experience. By the time of Mark's Gospel, Rome has seen the investiture of nine emperors, four of them during 68 and 69 CE (a precarious time for emperors!). By as early as 54 CE, the procession following the investiture of the emperor culminates in his deification. Here are some details, all from Schmidt 1997.

The rite begins in the *praetorium*, generally the residence of any high Roman official, but here the location of the imperial guard. First, the emperor is clothed in purple, a color only the highest classes in Rome may wear, the color of royalty and divinity. He is crowned with laurels and handed a staff representing power. Already, he resembles the statue of Jupiter in the temple of Jupiter Capitolinus where the procession culminates. The Praetorian Guard gather around him, shouting his praise, as the patronage system encourages them to do.

As the procession begins to wind its way along the Roman streets, a bull accompanies it, dressed in a manner similar to the emperor, and also crowned. Beside the bull walks a man carrying a two-headed ax, the instrument of sacrifice. Near the end of the procession, the emperor is offered a cup of wine, which he refuses, then pours out as a libation. The high point is the sacrifice that accompanies the emperor's enthronement and deification. These all take place at the temple of Jupiter on the Capitoline hill, the location where once a skull was found, said to indicate that Rome is to be head of all Italy. The place of enthronement is raised above the crowd.

Two emperors choose to be enthroned between other men, Tiberius between two consuls in 37 CE and Vitellius between two of his generals in 68 CE. Two generals also have a man on either side during their triumphal celebration. Claudius is physically supported between his sons-in-law in 44, and Vespasian celebrates his triumph over the Jews in 71 riding between Titus and Domitian. Claudius is already emperor. The other three later become emperors.

Here is Mark's Jesus. A whole cohort of soldiers (about two hundren men) leads him into the *praetorium* where they clothe him in purple and crown him with thorns. They then greet him with shouts of "Emperor of the Jews," kneel before him, and hit him with a staff. As the procession through the city begins, they make Simon of Cyrene walk with him, carrying the cross on which he is to be crucified. They offer Jesus wine, but he refuses it. He is crucified between two bandits. The place of the crucifixion is called the place of the skull. His cross raises Jesus above the crowd.

These details can hardly be historical. Jesus' crucifixion does not require two hundred soldiers. There is a pun on *praetorium*, which is the courtyard of the governor, but also the location of the emperor's elite troops, the Praetorian Guard, and the place from which the Roman emperors' processions begin. Only Pilate would have owned the purple clothing reserved for the highest classes, and he would never have lent it to clothe a criminal.

Some scholars think Simon of Cyrene is Mark's invention, merely the realistic detail a good storyteller might add. But when viewed through the lens of imperial processions, Simon is the man who carries the two-headed ax, the ax/cross being the instrument of sacrifice. Jesus and the emperor both refuse wine, hardly something normally offered to a criminal. The crucifixion raises Jesus above the crowd. It is his enthronement. (There is a pun here in Greek because the same word means "crucified" and "raised up." It is a pun John often employs.)

Mark's narrative is ironic, rich, and brilliant. In it, four things happen simultaneously. First is the literal narrative, the "history." Second is the enthronement and deification of Jesus as god-emperor, ruler of the world. Third, Jesus himself is the sacrifice that makes his own deification possible. Fourth is mockery of the investiture, procession, enthronement, and deification of the Roman emperor. The message is clear. Jesus is the true god-emperor, whereas the Roman emperor is a false god, an idol. This is the same kind of irony Mark employs earlier, in Jesus' triumphal entry into Jerusalem on a donkey, which can be read not only as mocking the Jewish revolutionaries, but also ridiculing the Romans who habitually make triumphal processions on horseback into cities they have conquered. The detail of the bandits crucified on either side of Jesus must have sent the Gentile readers of Mark's Gospel into paroxysms of laughter. What a way to mock Roman generals and future emperors, some of whom were far greater bandits than any ever crucified by Rome!

Paul's portrait

Paul has a peculiar saying at 2 Corinthians 2:14a that reflects Mark's theme. "Christ always leads us in triumphal procession," says Paul. Here, again, is Jesus as the Roman emperor at the head of a celebratory pageant. Paul is writing around 55, fifteen or more years before Mark, about twenty years after Jesus' death and as many after the emperor Gaius Caligula became a god in his own lifetime.

Thus, the idea of comparing Jesus to the Roman god-emperor occurs early in the Jesus movement. However, neither the extent nor the significance of the comparison in the Gospels and Paul has been appreciated until recently because the magnitude of the cult of Augustus was unknown. The cult of Caesar was thought to be only one among many, rather than the central cult of the empire. Through archaeological evidence and inscriptions, we now know that it pervades the Roman Empire by the time of Jesus' death. All over the empire, people can hardly go into public places without being reminded of it.

Paul treats the comparison somewhat as Mark does later. Both make a double claim. First, Jesus fulfills the Hebrew Scriptures. For Paul, the Jesus movement is the true Judaism, and those Jews who fail to convert are following matters of "the flesh," depending on kinship and their claim to the land, rather than living in "the Spirit."

Second, Jesus subverts Rome's claim that its emperor is savior, benefactor, and son of god. These titles belong not to Caesar but to Jesus, the true savior and ruler of the world. Rome's rule is parody.

But Paul's letter adds a radical interpretation. To suggest Jesus is an emperor just as divine as the man enthroned in Rome might say that the man in Rome is merely human and his trappings of divinity pretensions. But Paul not only equates Jesus with the god-emperor; he equates Jesus with Yahweh, the God of the Jews. This equation occurs as early as 54 in his letter to the Philippians, in a passage that echoes Isaiah 45:21-23. In the Isaiah passage, God is speaking:

> There is no other god besides me
> A righteous God and a Savior:
> There is no one besides me.
> ....
> from my mouth has gone forth in righteousness
> a word that shall not return:
> "To me every knee shall bow,
> every tongue shall swear."

Here is Philippians 2:10-11:

> At the name of Jesus
> Every knee should bend,
> In heaven and on earth and under the earth,
> And every tongue should confess
> That Jesus Christ is Lord.

Here, Jesus receives the honor and worship due to God. Scholars think Paul is here reproducing a hymn familiar in the Jesus movement. If so, the equation of Jesus with Yahweh antedates Paul's letter. It is easy to see why the early Christians might have compared a resurrected man with the emperor, especially in parody of the emperor's claims to be savior, liberator, and son of god. To equate Jesus with Yahweh is a different matter entirely. The equation flows from the Septuagint.

Wanting to know about Jesus, literate Greek-speaking Christians turn to the Septuagint, the Scriptures they believe Jesus has fulfilled. There references to God use neither "Yahweh," which is Hebrew, nor a Greek equivalent, but the Greek for "Lord." They already believe Jesus is Lord, so when they find "Lord" in the Septuagint, they interpret it as a reference to Jesus as God.

Moreover, that the Septuagint refers to Jesus as present at the time the original text was written implies that he exists before his birth to Mary. If he pre-exists, it must be in heaven, and if in heaven, then he not only ascends from earth to heaven, as in the interpretation of the synoptics, he also descends from heaven to earth, as in Paul and, later, John. If in heaven he is more exalted than the angels (Heb 1:4), the only Greek category left for him is *logos*. The *logos* is the divine power existing from the beginning with God who creates and orders the cosmos according to divine law. If Jesus is the *logos*, he is divine, deserving the honor and worship due to God.

In this way, people's mode of thinking about Jesus moves across cultures, and the cultures stimulate each other. The movement begins very soon after Jesus' death, starting before 54 when Paul writes his letter to the Philippians, and culminating somewhere in the 90s with John's Gospel. It is a small step from here to the Trinitarian formula of the Council of Nicaea in 325 and the two-natures Christology of the Council of Chalcedon in 451.

Implications

Christianity begins in Galilee with a poor Jewish peasant named Jesus seeking God through the movement led by John the Baptist. Before long, both are dead: John beheaded, Jesus crucified. Soon after Jesus' death, some of his followers think God raises Jesus from the dead. Because resurrection of the dead is one of the signs of the fulfillment of the dream of the end time, they think the end of the age is imminent. They think Jesus has ascended to heaven. He will return quickly as the heavenly

Messiah, leading angelic armies in a war against the unrighteous and against Rome, just as the dream predicts.

But Jesus does not return. Because he does not play the role of the traditional, militant, Davidic Messiah in his lifetime and because he does not return after death as the heavenly Messiah of Daniel 7, most Jews remain skeptical of Jesus' messianic status. He simply does not fit into Jewish categories, except that of failed messianic pretender, an all-too-familiar role for pious and ambitious Jewish men in the two first centuries. However, Greek-speaking Gentiles convert in droves, many having been God-fearers, already attending synagogues in the Diaspora, active in Jewish life, but unwilling to undergo circumcision or fully adhere to Torah law. The new Jewish faction, which demands neither circumcision nor full adherence to Torah, appeals to them.

Thus, Greek influence enters the Jesus movement early and soon becomes dominant. Greek-speaking Romans already have categories of thought into which Jesus fits. He fits into the cult of the emperor. A dead man resurrected surely becomes a god, much as Julius and Augustus become gods after their deaths. They are also sons of gods. Jesus, being Jewish, must be the son of the Jewish God. In raising him from the dead, God vindicates him, placing him above the angels who have not suffered and died as Jesus has. In Greek philosophical thought, the category above the angels is that of *logos*. So, Jesus must have been the incarnate *logos,* with God from the beginning. This fits nicely with references to him as "Lord" in the Septuagint.

The Septuagint helps bridge the gap between Jewish and Greek thought, just as it does for Philo. Jesus can be the Jewish Messiah of Davidic ancestry, a Messiah born in David's city of Bethlehem. He is never the anticipated military leader. Indeed, he dies a painful and ignominious death. Hence, Christians transform the traditional militant Messiah into Isaiah's suffering servant and proclaim traditional Jewish expectations erroneous.

Jesus can also be the son of man of Daniel 7, the heavenly Messiah about to return at the head of angelic armies. His return is delayed, but he is enthroned in heaven. Like the heavenly Messiah, to him is given dominion, glory, and everlasting rule. Enthroned in heaven with dominion, glory, and everlasting rule, he can be the Greek *logos,* existing with God from all eternity and therefore, in the words of the Nicene Creed, "begotten, not created." Not having been created, he is "of one substance with the Father" to quote the Nicene Creed once more. As the *logos,* he is also recognizably the Lord referred to in the Septuagint, the creative word of God. Thus, thought comes full circle and Jew and Greek are reconciled, as Ephesians 2:11-22 proclaims.

The history of these ideas is not as neat as this brief reconstruction, of course. This has been a logical reconstruction, which passes swiftly from about 50 CE to 325 and 451. Nonetheless, something very like this does happen intellectually, as a person unlike the expected Davidic Messiah is transformed into the Davidic Messiah and the Son of Man Messiah simultaneously. Meanwhile, he is also transformed into the deified Roman emperor, son of a god, and the Greek *logos,* son of God. If the two cultures had not found common elements, Christianity would have been a different religion from that which conquered the Roman empire in the fourth century CE. If it had not borrowed powerful elements from Greek and Roman thought, it might not have lasted that long.

The central implication of this reconstructed history is that Jesus, the son of Mary, preacher, exorcist, and healer, is very different from Jesus, Messiah, Emperor, *Logos,* Son of God. The difference is not primarily that the Galilean preacher is human, but the *logos* divine (a complex issue I address in Chapter 11). The difference lies in the message conveyed. Jesus the Galilean peasant is a person of this world, healing in this world, reconciling in this world, behaving toward others with equality and inclusiveness. He mocks the other worldly dream, the dream of the end time when everyone will do homage to the Jewish God in the Jewish Temple, and the old kinship clans and the ancient land will be restored. In Paul's terms, this dependence on kinship, buildings, and possessions is following "the flesh," an interesting twist because "the flesh," which in Paul seems so worldly, is an otherworldly dream. Jesus will have none of it. He rejects its arrogant exclusiveness and hatred of others.

If this interpretation of Jesus is right and Jesus' message is true, God's empire is already here. God is always present and always breaking through. He is seen in healing and the reconciliation brought to all through the forgiveness of sins. Our forgiveness of others brings peace to humanity. God's forgiveness of us makes peace between us and God. If this message is Jesus' message, then to follow Jesus is to do as he has done, here and now. We are to search out our own sin and repent, to heal and reconcile, love and forgive, with adjustments, of course, for the vast differences between his culture and ours about what needs reconciliation and love. But now as then, to exclude others and to condemn them as wicked or unworthy is sin.

If the historical Jesus is taken seriously and worshiped by imitation, his worshipers will concern themselves with the reform of this world, with bringing about compassion and inclusiveness, here and now. On the other hand, if Jesus is worshiped as *logos* while his life is ignored, worship of him can be abstracted, ritualized, and removed from the concerns of this world. His worshipers will pray to him for miracles rather than making miracles happen themselves. If his divinity is emphasized to the exclusion of his humanity, doing as he did becomes impossible. We are not divine. How can we do what divinity once did? Better to follow someone else, to adopt the way of Dominic as the Roman Catholic order of Dominicans does or the way of Francis of Assisi as Franciscans do. Or follow Luther or Calvin or Billy Graham or…anyone but Jesus.

So one way Christianity has gone wrong is to have reconstructed Jesus to fit existing concepts from Jewish, Roman, and Greek culture and to have de-emphasized the message the historical Jesus brings. The next chapter argues that Christianity has also misunderstood Jesus' death

9 | *Jesus' Death*

The causes

The Romans crucify Jesus outside the walls of Jerusalem while Pontius Pilate is governor. This is the best-established fact about Jesus. It is impossible to be certain of the reason for his crucifixion. The Romans crucify thousands of Jews in the first century CE. Pilate is notoriously cruel in a brutal world, and he crucifies some people without trial. Galileans are famous among a rebellious people for their defiance and lawlessness. Perhaps there was no reason. Perhaps Pilate did not want to bother with the case of yet another Galilean Jew and called a centurion to flog and crucify him without trial.

On the other hand, the Romans are proud of their system of justice. They dedicate a temple to justice in Rome. They believe in the rule of law. They are not known for grabbing just anyone off the street and crucifying him for fun.

The authorities at the Temple collaborate with the Romans. Above all, both groups want to keep the peace in Jerusalem. The Temple authorities also want to keep the Temple functioning, for it provides their livelihood. Moreover, they are believing Jews. They think a Temple managed according to Torah law is the will of God, and they do whatever must be done to see that the Temple operates smoothly.

The Torah demands the sacrifice of unblemished animals, and the Temple keeps herds and flocks of animals suitable for sacrifice. This is not merely a business proposition. People coming from a distance are not able to bring an animal with them. Keeping it unblemished is difficult, keeping it fed and watered a hardship. So people come to the Temple carrying money, and there they buy animals to sacrifice.

No universal currency exists. Many cities mint their own coins. Since the time of Julius Caesar, the emperor's image is on many of the coins as a god or a son of god. Other coins carry images of Roman gods who have never been human. To Jews, these are idols. A Jew cannot use money with idols on it for buying and selling in the Temple. For all these reasons, the Temple has moneychangers and animals to be bought and sold. They are necessary if the Temple is to function at all.

There is no evidence that this system is corrupt in Jesus' time. Those who complain of corruption protest the illegitimate ancestry of the reigning priesthood or an incorrect calendar for festivals, not buying and selling in the Temple.

The Temple incident is not primarily a protest against commercialism. Jesus' actions are symbolic. They are against attention to ritual that distracts from attention to God, against the militants whose hatreds are ripping Judaism asunder and will cause its downfall, and against the dream of the end time. Jesus predicts the total destruction of the Temple, something almost anyone with insight into human nature could anticipate if the militants keep rebelling against Rome.

Jesus' behavior angers and frightens the Temple authorities. They may well have already been angry because Jesus, like John the Baptist, proclaims forgiveness of sins outside the Temple system. He also speaks of God's presence in Galilee. According to Jewish belief, God is most fully present in the Holy of Holies, the inner sanctum of the Temple. The power of God's presence decreases with distance from that spot. Galilee is far away. The authorities may think Jesus is undermining the power, and perhaps the holiness, of the Temple. The Temple authorities are probably not much disturbed by his failure to keep the purity laws, about which Galileans are notoriously lax, anyway. Local authorities might have felt more threatened by the sense of chaos, the breaking of boundaries that seems to accompany Jesus wherever he goes.

Even in Galilee, Jesus is a troublemaker. Then he arrives in Jerusalem and causes a disturbance in the Temple when the city is crowded with those going to the festival of Passover, the most popular of the Jewish festivals, the festival of Jewish liberation. Tensions are already high. Above all, the authorities want to keep the peace. They have solid reasons to arrest Jesus and to exclude him from the festival. The easiest way to remove him is to hand him over to the Romans, who will eliminate him permanently.

The Romans also want to keep the peace, and they do not mind crucifying troublemakers. They may have heard that Jesus speaks about the empire of God in contrast to that of Rome and has predicted or threatened the destruction of the Temple, or even of Jerusalem. To them, he sounds like another Jewish militant. Time to eradicate him before he gathers an army and they have to call out the troops, as they have had to do before.

Everyone in power feels safer with Jesus exterminated. So they crucify him in standard Roman manner, flogging him first, writing his crime on a plaque, and keeping people away from the cross. The plaque could well have read "Emperor of the Jews." This seems to be how the Romans interpret him, and perhaps this is the reason the Jewish authorities give for his arrest. Talk of an alternative empire plus talk of destruction adds up to rebellion against Rome. Jesus is not innocent in the sense that he must be framed to be found guilty. Both the Temple authorities and the Romans have genuine reasons to destroy him.

As judgment

The Hebrew Scriptures speak of the judgment of God in this world, in history. They treat the Exile as God's judgment on God's people. Later, the Jews begin to realize that history is not necessarily just, and the book of Daniel, written in the 160s BCE, locates justice in another world where God raises and judges the dead, sending the righteous to eternal life, the wicked to eternal condemnation (Dan 12:2).

Borrowing from the dream of the end time, Christian tradition also speaks of resurrection and a last judgment, with Jesus as judge. But Christianity has another tradition. The community around the author of John's Gospel believes that judgment occurs in this world, beginning with the appearance of Jesus. John 3:19 sums it up, "And this is the judgment, that the light has come into the world, and people loved darkness rather than light because their deeds were evil." John's idea is that people are judged now because of the locus of their love. Those who love darkness and practice evil have been judged and condemned already. Those who love light and do good works have been judged and redeemed already. To John, love of light means loving Jesus, who is the light of the world.

In such a tradition, Jesus' death brings judgment, a harsh and terrible judgment, because everyone involved is condemned. Most thoroughly accursed are the Temple authorities, for they are the ones who arrest Jesus and send him to the Romans for execution. They are, of course, both rich and members of a faction, groups Jesus has castigated all along. They fail to show compassion, while making forgiveness of sins depend on the ability to buy and sacrifice animals. They also consider themselves righteous, for they possess all the components of righteousness—wealth, power, and strict adherence to Torah, in contrast to the Pharisees who add oral laws to sacred Scripture.

The Romans are condemned, too, for they execute Jesus. However, they seem oddly innocent, unsuspectingly caught up in something they do not understand. This is the judgment of the Gospel writers who are trying to attract Romans to the new Jewish faction, but it is substantiated by historical research. The Jewish authorities understand and condemn, if they know Jesus is mocking the dream of the end time. The Romans misinterpret.

Yet the condemnation is much broader than this group of Jews or that group of Romans. Roman or Jew is not the issue. The issues are abuse of power and wealth, lack of compassion, exclusion, refusal to repent, and failure to forgive. This interpretation fits Jesus' teachings. Other cultures also stand condemned, including modern democracies that allow the concentration of wealth and power in a few hands, exploit the poor, lack compassion, refuse to repent of and change sinful social structures, and fail to forgive.

Everyone abandons Jesus. Peter, John, James, Mary, and the rest of the disciples flee for their lives, leaving Jesus to his fate. Is this, perhaps, a judgment on human nature itself—our fear of pain and death, our fear of social condemnation, our desire always to be in control? To stand and speak up for one's beliefs takes enormous courage. Most of us lack it, even if we have convictions.

Finally, Jesus' death judges the fickle crowds who love Jesus when he heals them and speaks of God's presence in their lives, but who are ready to run after other healers and exorcists, other "doers of wonderful works," when Jesus gets into trouble. Human nature comes out badly in the Gospels, so that Jesus' death judges us all. This makes his message of forgiveness all the more poignant.

As sacrifice for sin

The New Testament is replete with metaphors to interpret Jesus' death. They come from law (justification), slavery and commerce (redemption), sports and war (triumph), and human relations generally (reconciliation). But the most common relate to worship, and in the first century, worship means sacrifice. Thus, the most common understanding of Jesus' death is as a sacrifice. The idea seems already ripe in the earliest extant letter of Paul (1 Thess 4:10), and appears also in Colossians 1:14, Ephesians 1:7, and Matthew 26:28.

In Jewish thought, sacrifice dates to Cain and Abel, Noah, and the giving of the Torah. Later, Jews interpret the deaths of the Maccabbean martyrs of the 160s BCE as sacrificial. Greek and Roman life is filled with priests sacrificing animals to gods and goddesses in temples. Specialists who study sacrifice conclude that most sacrifices fall into three categories: those made in gratitude for favors granted, in petition for aid, and in repentance of sin.

Shocked by Jesus' unexpected and cruel death, his followers wonder why it happens. After his resurrection, they see Jesus in cosmic terms and seek cosmic answers. They agree that Jesus could not have been justly crucified, because his resurrection vindicates his death. Jesus' death could not have been in gratitude or petition, so they conclude that he died as a sacrifice for the forgiveness of sins, especially because their culture interprets the deaths of the righteous as sacrificial.

Jesus' words and deeds reinforce this conclusion. His followers recall that Jesus preached and practiced the forgiveness of sins. It is one of his central messages. It had been a constant theme of his mentor, John the Baptist.

It is important to emphasize that Jesus' followers, whether Jewish or Roman, could not have developed any other interpretation of Jesus' death. Death as sacrifice is in the air they breathe. It is their constant way of worship. It is part of their martyrological and heroic traditions. After Jesus' followers accept his resurrection, they find it transparently obvious that Jesus' death is a sacrifice for sins.

However, their interpretation poses a problem. It does not accord with Jesus' guiding vision. Repeatedly, Jesus declares that God has forgiven people's sins without requiring sacrifice. In the story of the Prodigal Son (Luke 15:11-24), the father (God) forgives the son immediately and orders a banquet of welcome for him. The evidence that Jesus thinks God forgives sins readily is so strong that one of the greatest Jesus scholars, E. P. Sanders (1993, p. 326), lists in his conclusion as "certain or virtually certain" that Jesus promises the empire of God to the wicked. I think Jesus promises God's empire to repentant sinners, not to the unrepentant, but he does not promise it to the righteous. From the point of view of the righteous, this would look like promising it to the wicked.

If Jesus does not consider sacrifice necessary for the forgiveness of sins, we are foolish at best and arrogant at worst to interpret his own death as a sacrifice for sin. The Gospel narratives of the Last Supper provide additional evidence that Jesus does not die for the forgiveness of sins.

The Last Supper

The Last Supper is the most thoroughly researched event in the New Testament and one of the least understood. At one extreme, scholars conclude that it is not a Passover meal; it has no passion symbolism; Jesus does not institute anything during it; during it, Jesus does not perform anything like the later Eucharist (Crossan 1991). At the other extreme, they conclude that Jesus institutes something very like the modern Eucharist as a vehicle of atonement for his followers here and now and a gift in anticipation of the end time (Jeremias 1966).

Interpreting the Last Supper is difficult for three reasons:

(1) Even if historically accurate, the material in the Gospels and Paul is too brief to convey the meaning of the meal. Moreover, the Gospel of John disagrees with the synoptics and with Paul, so historical accuracy is difficult to ascertain.

(2) Beyond these meager materials, a plethora of interpreta-

tive possibilities emerges. In speaking of body and blood, Jesus could have been referring to the sacrifice of Isaac, who dies in the Aramaic rendition of the Hebrew Scriptures with which Jesus may have been familiar. He could have been alluding to sacrifices in the Temple, or to the Passover sacrifices, or to those of Cain or Abel or Moses. He could have been anticipating his own death. Finally, he could have been suggesting nothing at all. Scholars have argued in favor of all these possibilities.

(3) Among Jesus' followers, celebration of the Last Supper begins early and happens often. The historical event quickly becomes buried beneath layers of liturgical tradition. That tradition soon enters the culture of Rome and falls under its influence. Conclusions about what is historical depend on how finely scholars sift the materials, with no agreed criteria for how coarse or fine the filter needs to be.

Nonetheless, many events and cultural perceptions linked to the Last Supper are well attested. Jesus eats with his followers, with sinners, and with strangers, all the time. This supper is the last only because Jesus dies before tomorrow's. His table fellowship is inclusive, and it is insulting both to those who keep purity laws and to those fighting and dying for the dream of the end time. Jesus' meals celebrate the empire of God, here and now. Jesus forgives sins without requiring sacrifice or Temple. Hosts of meals generally bless the bread and wine, so Jesus probably says the blessings. Jesus' actions are often symbolic. Jews abhor the idea of consuming blood because they think the blood of an animal belongs to God. To drink human blood, even symbolically, would be not only loathsome but also blasphemous. In contrast, consuming blood in the Gentile mystery cults represents a way to overcome death. And, finally, the Last Supper becomes a central Christian rite very early.

Shortly before the final supper, Jesus goes into the Temple and causes a commotion, objecting to at least some activities there. A Jew from the hinterlands of Galilee might well object that priests perform all the sacrifices, sacrifices once done by lay heads of household. Rabbi Hillel (30 BCE–9 CE), one of Jesus' most respected older contemporaries, raises precisely this objection.

Earlier, I have argued that Jesus often mocks the dream of the end time. Perhaps he also mocks the Temple sacrifices, which he, like John the Baptist before him, considers unnecessary. Perhaps, while eating supper with his disciples after the Temple incident, Jesus mockingly raises the bread and says, "*This* is my sacrifice, the body I bring to break at God's altar." Perhaps later he raises the wine, mockingly saying, "*This* is my sacrifice, the blood I bring to spill at God's altar." Or words to that effect.

In the Hebrew Scriptures, God rejects Cain's agricultural sacrifice, but accepts Abel's animal offering (Gen 4:3-5a). Here is Jesus, lifting up to God Cain's rejected agricultural sacrifice of grain and grape. He breaks the bread in lieu of killing an animal and drinks the wine instead of pouring out blood. Being a Jew, he would never have reinterpreted the wine as blood. His very point would have been that the wine is wine, not blood.

Such a parody of sacrificial worship, using Jesus' typical techniques of exaggeration and reversal, is quite funny, as Jesus' sayings and actions often are. Moreover, it is life affirming, as Jesus' banquets have always been. But here Jesus is not merely banqueting. He is mocking the means of other banquets, both Jewish and Roman. The meat people eat in the first century is sacrificed meat. To a Jew, to sacrifice is to kill as kosher, so the meat is pure, acceptable to God as an offering, to Jews as food. Jesus' kosher banquet of bread and wine does not need priests to kill it. It does not require the Temple rites. To the Temple authorities, priests all, this mockery and repudiation is highly insulting. Maybe this mockery is what Judas betrays. Maybe this is why the Temple authorities arrest Jesus and explains why he is not arrested immediately after the Temple incident. The Temple authorities tarry until a further provocation. Jesus' mockery of their central function provides it.

No matter how funny the disciples might have found this, and no matter how dangerous they may have felt it, after Jesus' death and resurrection, they reinterpret it. They reinterpret it not because they want to distort history, but because it takes on new meaning for them. I will speculate a little further about how this reinterpretation might have happened.

The first relevant event is the disciples' experience of Jesus' resurrection. Soon, they interpret his crucifixion in the light of his resurrection, as a sacrifice for sin.

Now, especially, the disciples want to remember Jesus, and because meals together constituted an important part of their relationship, they reenact the last meal as a memorial. In doing so, they recall Jesus' words about the bread and wine being *his* sacrifice, the sacrifice he brings before God, a substitute for animal sacrifices in the Temple.

But they no longer see the substitution as a joke. Jesus died, they think, as a sacrifice for sin, replacing Temple sacrifices. This must mean that this bread and this wine, as Jesus' sacrifice, represent his body and blood. Jesus must have been anticipating his own, sacrificial death. Thus, Paul can end his account of the institution of the Last Supper with these words, "For as often as you eat this bread and drink the cup, you proclaim the Lord's death until he comes" (1 Cor 11:26).

Whereas drinking blood, even symbolically, is anathema to Jews, Gentiles understand drinking blood during pagan sacrificial rites as a way to overcome death. Crucified, Jesus sheds his blood. Resurrected, he overcomes death. For Jesus' Gentile converts, symbolically drinking his blood now is participation in Jesus' conquest of death.

Moreover, this reenactment of the Last Supper is not an empty symbol. When the disciples reenact it, they experience Jesus' presence. Remembering that final supper and also their many other meals together with Jesus, they retrospectively interpret all their shared meals as revelatory. Thus, all the Gospels present Jesus as revealed to his disciples in meals he shares with them, both before and after his resurrection.

This interpretation fits nicely with the portrait of Jesus developed in this book. Jesus finds God everywhere, here, now, in this world, out in the desert, in the homes of sinners, in the daily provisions of food and water, in the birds of the air and the flowers of the field. God's empire is hidden, small, and precious. Often, it is mistaken for something evil.

Jesus symbolically mocks other guiding visions, for he thinks they lead people astray. He is especially harsh on the dream of the end time because it locates the human encounter with God in the wrong place, in the future and beyond this world. Moreover, it promotes arrogant blindness and the condemnation of others. The dream is destructive. It leads to the militancy that will call forth the wrath of the Romans who will annihilate the Jews, not the wrath of God who will restore the Jewish tribes to their land.

The Temple, too, puts God in the wrong place. It confines God in the Holy of Holies, approachable only by priests—men of the right kinship, men of landed wealth who collaborate with Rome to make the poor destitute. The Temple makes forgiveness of sins dependent on priests and on righteousness. Indeed, the Temple represents many of the things Jesus has already opposed in Galilee. He does not change when he comes up to Jerusalem. He praises and protests and mocks the same old things in the different guise they wear in Jerusalem.

Jesus' words and actions are consistent from the time of his baptism until his death. His guiding vision is of the empire of God, here and now. Its corollaries are the forgiveness of sins, here and now, and the inclusion in God's empire of all who repent. Because this is his guiding vision, Jesus mocks a very different vision, the dream of the end time with its arrogant factionalism whose hatreds are destroying Judaism. Jesus does not anticipate his sacrificial death at the final supper. He does not die as a sacrifice for sins. He believes God has forgiven our sins already, without sacrifice.

10 *Recapitulation*

The social context

Judaism is ailing in the two first centuries. It is fevered with factionalism and exclusiveness. Its unhealthiness emerges in civil wars, ethnic cleansing, forced religious conversions, and assassinations.

While factionalism and exclusiveness appear in other cultures, Judaism as practiced in the two first centuries facilitates them. The Jews are people of Torah, and most want to follow God's laws. Yet no authoritative body exists that has exclusive rights to interpret Torah. The result is that any charismatic figure with a new interpretation may develop a following and, if sufficiently large, that following becomes a faction.

Worse, Judaism lacks the tradition of rational skepticism so characteristic of the Roman Cynics. The Jewish factions are arrogant. Each faction thinks its interpretation of Torah is God's true word, its practices God's undoubted will, and its members righteous. Each faction thinks other interpretations unholy and other practices unrighteous.

The dream of the end time magnifies factionalism and arrogance. The dream says God sides with the righteous and will fling the fullness of divine wrath upon the wicked in a devastating war. In the end, God will vindicate the righteous and punish the wicked. When God's empire has arrived, a new Temple will descend from heaven, the righteous dead will be resurrected, the ancient tribes restored, and pagans flock to Jerusalem to worship the Jewish God. Even many Jews who are not members of factions dream this dream, for it represents Jewish hopes.

John the Baptist does not belong to a faction. He is another charismatic figure who creates one. He teaches that the fulfillment of the dream is imminent and preaches repentance, the forgiveness of sins, and conversion to righteousness.

Meanwhile, the Romans try to keep the peace. They recognize the religious rights of the Jews and even give them special privileges, for the Romans respect whatever is ancient, and Judaism is ancient. They try to include everyone in their empire and legalize the customary laws and practices of conquered nations. Into this world, Jesus of Nazareth is born. He speaks to its situation.

The unforgivable sin

The Gospels introduce Jesus as a follower of John the Baptist who accepts John's baptism. At his baptism, Jesus has a profound religious experience that drives him out into the desert. When he returns, he does not rejoin John. He does not speak of the empire of God as arriving in a wrathful war with the righteous or repentant saved and the wicked damned. He does not envision the empire of God as resembling that of ancient Judaism or contemporary Rome. He says little about the resurrection of the dead. He has seen differently.

He speaks of God's empire as small, hidden, precious, and present now, worth all a person has now, in this life. However, he is aware that not everyone sees it and that some who do see it think it evil. Those who deny it are either too busy with their own worldly affairs to notice or so proud of their righteousness that they reject it as unrighteous. Jesus is particularly hard on the latter group, for they represent the Jewish factions, the arrogant who are tearing Judaism apart. Jesus censures them for their sin of arrogance and condemnation of others while he forgives those who break the Ten Commandments and the other laws of Torah, probably because righteous factions cause more harm than wicked lawbreakers. Civil wars in which eight hundred opponents are crucified at once are far more harmful than individual theft and adultery. Assassination is premeditated murder. Riots against Rome entail a disturbance of agriculture that leads to famine. Righteous rebellion against Rome by the priests of the Temple eventually leads to the destruction of the Temple and Jerusalem.

The central reason the factions are so harmful is that their members are blind to their own sin. They see themselves as virtuous, as the sword of God slaying the wicked in God's righteous war. In contrast, those who break the Ten Commandments know they are sinners in need of God's mercy.

The contrast between the tremendous harm caused by the righteous and the small harm by the wicked becomes even more vivid in the twentieth century. Adolph Hitler, the vegetarian who declined alcohol and abhorred personal violence, followed the laws of his faction religiously and thereby caused the torture and death of tens of millions, hundreds of millions if the war dead are counted. Jeffrey Dahmer was an alcoholic homosexual who stalked homosexuals, then seduced, murdered, and ate them—certainly one of the wicked. He killed seventeen.

It is the righteous who commit the unforgivable sin. When they see God's empire of mercy and compassion, they reject it as unrighteous because it does not vindicate them and condemn their enemies. When asked to repent, they say they have obeyed the law and do not need to repent. They refuse to come into the banquet God prepares for them. Their sin cannot be forgiven because they do not accept forgiveness, although it is offered to them.

The Christian Gospels present the Pharisees as the arrogant, but the Gospels are written after 70 CE when the Temple is burned, the Sadducees gone, the Essenes' main settlement destroyed.

and most of the Sicarii and Zealots dead or enslaved. Jewish fratricide has left only the Pharisees as a strong threat against the Christians. In Jesus' day, all the factions still exist. Jesus condemns them all, perhaps especially the Essenes who despise their enemies and daily prepare for the holy war of the end time.

The empire of God

Jesus thinks the end time dream is a hallucination, and he begs the dreamers to open their eyes to the empire of God spread all around them, precious, present, and accessible now. God's empire as Jesus sees it is a reverse image of the empire dreamed of by the factions.

The dream speaks of hating one's foes. Jesus calls people to love their enemies and pray for their persecutors. The dream speaks of war and destruction. Jesus calls for peace and bounteous growth, like that of a mustard seed springing into leaf or yeast making bread rise. The dream is of exclusion. Jesus is inclusive. The dream cries for the vindication of the righteous. Jesus tells of the exoneration of sinners. The dream longs for God's justice. Jesus trusts God's mercy. The dream tells of the end of sickness and disease someday. Jesus heals the sick and diseased now. The dream launches God's empire through holy war. Jesus reveals God's empire through healing and forgiveness. The dream envisions the restoration of kinship and the natural hierarchy families entail. Jesus decries kinship and embraces the egalitarianism of friendship. The dream is of the restoration of the Holy Land to the Jews. Jesus is an itinerant without possessions. The dream anticipates a new, heavenly Temple. Jesus ignores the Temple and, perhaps, mocks its functions.

In the conclusion to his great work, *Jesus and Judaism*, E. P. Sanders lists things that are "certain or virtually certain" about Jesus, then descends through the less certain to those that are "incredible." Among the "incredible" is that Jesus "believed in love, mercy, grace, repentance and the forgiveness of sin" and that "Jews...would kill people who believed in such things" (1985, 326-327). Stated this baldly and without context, of course. Sanders is right. But in context, the incredible becomes horribly creditable. Preaching love of Pharisees to Essenes who hate them, mercy toward collaborators to Sicarii who assassinate them, prayer for Romans to the priests who suspend the sacrifices for them, peace to Zealots who war against Rome, and repentance to righteous keepers of Torah, might well have been hazardous to the speaker's health. Jesus died partly for mocking the end time dream that symbolized so many Jewish hopes and Roman fears.

New dreams

Jesus mocks the dream of the end time and perhaps ridicules the Temple. The Jews understand that he is derisive while the Romans take him seriously. This is a lethal combination.

Soon after his death, his followers proclaim his resurrection. According to the dream of the end time, resurrection is a sign of the vindication of the righteous. His followers thus classify Jesus as one of the righteous. The crucifixion of the righteous needs explanation. Judaism has a tradition of the martyrdom of the righteous as a sacrifice. Jew and pagan alike atone for sin by sacrifice. Jesus spoke constantly of the forgiveness of sin. So, his followers conclude that his death must have been a sacrifice for sin, although Jesus found sacrifices for sin unnecessary.

Resurrection is also a sign of the imminent fulfillment of the dream of the end time. Jesus has been resurrected and ascends to heaven. Therefore, his followers think he will come again soon, at the end of the age, this time as the heavenly Messiah who will lead God's holy war against the Romans and the wicked. If Jesus is the Messiah in heaven, he must have been the Messiah on earth, the Davidic Messiah, later transformed into the suffering servant. Such are post-resurrection dreams among Jesus' Jewish followers.

Gentiles dream of human beings ascending to heaven to be with the gods. All the emperors go to the gods in heaven when they die, just as Julius Caesar did. Like the emperors, Jesus is in heaven. On earth, emperors are sons of gods. On earth, Jesus must have been the Son of the Jewish God.

In heaven, the Gentile *logos* is begotten of God and above all other beings but God. In heaven, Jesus is above the angels, higher than all other beings but God. Jesus must be the *logos*. On earth, Jesus must have been the *logos* incarnate.

And, so, the Jewish dream of the end time, which dies after the failure of the bar Kochba rebellion in 135, is reborn in Jesus' resurrection and merged with Gentile longings to become a new religion, Christianity, which conquers Rome in 313 through the emperor Constantine (~280-337). Jesus was not a Christian. Christianity is his legacy, but not his vision.

After the destruction of the Jewish factions in 70, Jesus' followers forget about the factionalism Jesus denounces. Ironically, they become a new faction themselves, ready to assert the truth of their beliefs against the Pharisees. As Jesus' followers separate from Judaism, they themselves break into factions. Paul complains of the fracturing of the Corinthian assembly where some claim descent from Paul, some from Apollos, and some from Cephas (1 Cor 1:12). Soon, there is a faction of Christian Gnostics.

In later centuries, Arians fight Trinitarians and Catholics split from the Orthodox. At the Reformation, Reformers battle Catholics, then break into factions themselves. During the Great Awakening, Methodists separate from Anglicans. In our own day, there are some thirty-three thousand Christians factions arguing over interpretations of the Bible, just as Jews of the two first centuries and Israelis today argue over the Torah. Perhaps it is time for Jews and Christians to repudiate their dreams and imitate Jesus, whom Jews revere as a prophet and Christians claim to worship.

ACTIONS

This part of the book vaults from the first century to the twenty-first. It applies the knowledge and interpretations of Jesus presented in Chapters 2-10 to beliefs and actions today. It suggests how people in the twenty-first century may legitimately think about Jesus and suggests some ways to imitate him.

Chapter 11 draws on my own background in philosophy of science. It argues that we need to abandon many of the ways we have thought about Jesus, for they are no longer tenable. It also suggests new ways to think about him that do not conflict with science. Chapter 12 makes proposals for daily living in imitation of Jesus. A brief conclusion ends the book.

11 | Repudiate the Dreams

Messiah, emperor, *logos*

People in the two first centuries live in cultures very different from our own. First century converts to Christianity fit Jesus into the guiding beliefs of their cultures. They understand Jesus in their own terms, the only terms they have.

The Jews have two central concepts of a coming Messiah. One is an earthly military emperor like David who will free the Jews from the Roman yoke and liberate the land. The other is a heavenly Messiah who will arrive at the head of angelic armies and be victorious in the final war between the righteous and unrighteous. After Jesus' resurrection, his followers give him both these roles.

Those Jews who accept Jesus' resurrection dream again the dream of the imminent end time. But the end time never comes. It is a fantasy, as Jesus knew.

The Gentiles to whom Paul preaches hear "resurrected and ascended," "lord," "savior," "peacemaker," and "son of God," and recognize these titles from the emperor cult. For Gentile converts, Jesus is their true emperor and lord.

Once Gentiles accept Jesus as emperor and lord, they look for these terms as they search the Septuagint for details about Jesus' life. Here they find "lord" and interpret it as *logos*. The *logos* preexists all else but God and is God's creative word. Jesus must have these characteristics, too.

Like a magnet, the resurrected Jesus attracts all these concepts from the cultures around him. His followers give him these roles. They are not concepts Jesus applies to himself. They are not concepts people in our culture understand. We do not anoint our leaders, we elect them. Our leaders do not come from God or the gods. They are human, like us. The Roman emperor who was lord and savior of the world vanishes with the fall of the Roman Empire in 476 CE. The literal emperor, metaphor for Jesus, disappears.

Once fully alive and applied to Jesus, these concepts are now empty and dead. They merely function as definitions that have come to us from long ago and far away. It is time to find some new, living concepts to apply to the resurrected Jesus. An interesting exercise might be to sit a few minutes and think of Jesus as you know him in your life, here and now, rather than from the metaphors used for him in the New Testament.

When I do this, those first century concepts melt away. They are not part of my life and do not capture my experience of Jesus. If I had only one adjective to describe my experience of Jesus, it would be *humble*, humble enough to seek me, forgive me, and liberate me. A necessary corollary to liberation has been judgment. However, Jesus' judgment does not resemble that of some external, feared authority. It is more like revelation. It always leads me to judge myself, either negatively or positively. It is always a step toward my salvation, liberation, and ability to love more fully.

Our relationship rests in freedom and mutuality. Most of all, Jesus wants to give himself to me, and for me to give myself to him in return. Jesus' love has liberated me from the acquisitive status-seeking that so dominates our culture. It has freed me from the racism of my childhood in the South and the homophobia pervading Christianity. It has healed me. From my own experience, I would characterize the risen Jesus as lover, liberator, healer.

and revealer. These characterizations have much in common with the scholars' portrait of the historical Jesus who reveals God's empire, liberates dreamers from fantasies of hatred and revenge, heals the sick, and loves the rejected. Characterizing Jesus as liberator, lover, healer, and revealer frees him from concepts tied to first century culture like Messiah, emperor, and *logos*.

Born of a virgin

The idea that Jesus is born of a virgin is also embedded in first century culture. Matthew 1:23 quotes Isaiah 7:14 from the Septuagint saying, "Look, the virgin shall conceive and bear a son,/ and they shall name him Emmanuel." The original Hebrew version of Isaiah uses the Hebrew word for a young woman of marriageable age, in contrast to the Hebrew word for a woman who has not had sexual intercourse. The Septuagint translates the former as the latter. The Gospel writers use the Septuagint's mistranslation, which the King James version of the Bible carries over into English as "virgin," retained in the NRSV quoted above.

Given this history, it is fascinating to find on Roman tombstones epitaphs to so-and-so, beloved wife of so-and-so and virgin mother of three! The Romans who wrote the epitaphs did not think the gods had been visiting. They used "virgin" more widely than we do to indicate a woman who is unlikely to conceive because her menstrual periods have not yet begun or have ceased with age. A virgin mother of three might have married before menarche and gotten pregnant with her first ovulation, borne two more children so rapidly that she did not menstruate between pregnancies, then died.

The curious concept of virgin birth meanders further. The Greek view of conception claims that the man gives the human spirit to the new child, whereas the woman gives it flesh. The Hebrew concept is similar. In it, the man supplies the seed, the woman the womb or soil in which it is nurtured. The agricultural analogy is obvious.

Both these ideas are natural and intuitive. Before the invention of the microscope, no one had seen sperm, but people could see wombs and menstruation. The man's contribution to conception must have seemed spiritual because invisible or formless, the woman's material because visible and tangible. Given these beliefs, it makes perfect sense to say that the man supplies the spirit/spiritual seed, the woman the flesh/soil/nurturance. Someone who held either belief would find it a matter of mere logic that spiritual beings can impregnate women. In such a union, the child receives the spirit of the spiritual being/god rather than a human spirit and acquires its flesh from its mother. Simple enough.

The Greeks and Romans already know that heroes are sons of thc gods who join the gods after death. The Jews have a concept of a son of God in human form. The cultural ground is ripe for Jesus to be born of a virgin, to be literally Son of God.

Contemporary biology draws a different picture. Here, the man provides half the child's DNA, a material string of chemicals. The woman contributes her half of DNA, also a material string of chemicals. These two bundles of DNA, the sperm and the egg, unite to form a zygote. If attached to the uterus, and without further complications, the zygote will grow into a fetus and be born as a child. If the zygote has a Y chromosome, the child will be male, if an X instead, female. Simple enough.

The difficulty for Christianity's belief in Jesus' virgin birth is that the first century concepts and twenty-first century science are incompatible. One cannot be translated into the language of the other. A first century spirit is not a string of chemical compounds, and chemical compounds are not spirits. Under contemporary biology, the virgin birth of Jesus is not conceptually possible (no pun intended).

Because the problem is conceptual and logical rather than factual, calling on miracles to save the virgin birth will not help.

If Jesus is to be divine as conceptualized in the early Christian centuries, he needs half his DNA and a Y chromosome from God that is *of God's substance*, exactly the same thing God is made of, whatever that is. Whatever it is, it is not DNA. Here is insurmountable incompatibility between donor and recipient! The incompatibility is logical. This is philosophy's insolvable mind/ body problem in an unusual guise. Once contemporary science replaces Greek and Hebrew thought, a virgin birth such as envisioned for Jesus is not possible. This does not negate Jesus' divinity differently conceived, an issue discussed in the final section of this chapter. Before this issue can be addressed, the Greek concepts of essence and person need examination.

Essences and persons

The idea that biological species have essences goes back to Plato and Aristotle (384-322 BCE). An essence is unchanging and makes something what it is. The idea that species have essences has a tenacious grip on the human mind. It is intuitive. And it is wrong.

The realization in biology that species do not have essences goes back to Charles Darwin (1809-1882). He argues (correctly) that biological species change. They evolve and either become new species over time or bud off new species while the old one continues to exist. Every biological species is mutable, which means none has an essence. The human species is no exception. That humanity does not have an essence affects theological arguments about Jesus.

In definitions dating to the important Christian councils of Nicaea (325) and Chalcedon (451), Jesus has two essences, divine and human. According to the Athanasian Creed (~ 400), when Jesus ascends, he takes his human essence into the divine realm.

In Jesus, the human essence and the divine essence are so intermixed that he is a single person, a fully unified being.

If there is no human essence, this philosophical method of uniting the divine and human in Jesus fails. When today's concepts are substituted, the method still fails. People often consider DNA a kind of essence. If Jesus' resuscitated body gets to heaven, wherever that is, Jesus would arrive with DNA that is uniquely his, yet in part shared with every organism on earth. By definition, DNA cannot constitute the essence of a species, which must be unique to a species and common to every member of it.

The Greek idea of person depends on the concept of essence. According to this idea, each individual has a unique essence. If so, it is hard to understand how Jesus can be one person, but two essences, the Trinity three persons, but one essence. These concepts have always been puzzling, but they also once did a lot of philosophical work. With the rise of contemporary science, they no longer serve any function at all. Rather, they inhibit our understanding of how God and a human being can be united.

They drag us away from the understanding of humanity provided by the fact that human beings evolved. The theory of evolution says our basic and essential drives are for reproduction and resources, and that we can transcend them. The fulcrum is love, the love evolution gives us for our kin. Evolution often uses a characteristic evolved for one purpose to fulfill another. Our narrow love of kin can widen to love of God, neighbor, and even enemies. Often our love widens through metaphors that speak of kinship. They say God is our father and other people are our brothers and sisters. Such widened love unites a person to God, who is Love. Rather than the philosophical language of essences and persons, we need a scientifically oriented language if we are to speak meaningfully today about Jesus' being both human and divine.

Human and divine

We know neither what makes us human nor what makes God divine. How difficult, then, to try to speak of what makes Jesus both human and divine!

The best road to take may be to listen to the mystics. We know they are human, and our knowledge of their relationships to God tells us they are "spirit persons," like Jesus, people filled with the spirit of God. Any list of great mystics must include the author of *The Cloud of Unknowing*, Brother Lawrence, Francis of Assisi, John of the Cross, Teresa, Jacob Boehme, William Blake, George Fox, John Woolman, Thomas Merton, Buddha, and the Zen, Sufi, and Kabalistic masters. In very different languages, all speak of the same things. They tell of their unity with God after tremendous spiritual struggles. They tell us that the apparently separate entities all around us are united as one, that we do not have separate selves, but are related to each other and to everything else in the universe. (Interestingly, contemporary science has arrived at approximately the same conclusion by a completely different route.) They treat others with the compassion that springs from this knowledge. All are certain of permanent union with the One/God, and they know that union now.

Most go on some sort of spiritual quest. Prince Buddha leaves home and wealth to fast so enthusiastically his hair falls out before he realizes that extreme asceticism is not the path to enlightenment. He meditates and, reaching enlightenment, shares his knowledge with others. He teaches a new way of seeing the world and an end to suffering for those who relinquish egocentricity and personal desire.

Jesus has an experience of enlightenment at his baptism that drives him out into the wilderness to consider its meaning. When he returns, he begins a movement surprisingly similar to Buddha's, given the differences in their cultures and social standing. Both teach new ways of seeing. Both disparage worldly goods and social status, ego and arrogance. Both teach humility and compassion. Such teachings come from people filled with God's spirit.

To be filled with God, then, is to know oneself inseparable from God and God's universe. To be filled with God is to embody divine compassion and forgiveness, to lay aside the egocentric concerns of this world for far greater treasure. Matthew's version of Jesus' summary of the way to such fulfillment is, "You shall love the Lord your God with all your heart, and with all your soul, and with all your mind...[and] your neighbor as yourself" (Matt 22:37-40).

Without the Greek and Hebrew metaphors Christianity uses to characterize Jesus, what remains is the mystic. Jesus is a human being who goes on a spiritual quest. We know nothing about that quest until we meet Jesus at his baptism. Here, Jesus is filled so completely with God's spirit, feels himself so close to God, that the only metaphor appropriate is "son." Later, Jesus will extend this metaphor by calling God *"Abba,"* an intimate term roughly the equivalent of our "daddy."

Filled with God's spirit, Jesus has seen God's empire. He says it is small and hidden, but worth all one has. To find it, people must seek it. Jesus has known God's forgiveness. He says sacrifice and purity are unnecessary. Only our arrogance stands between us and God's mercy. This unforgivable arrogance is that of the righteous who obey, work hard, keep the laws, and long for a justice that vindicates them and condemns the wicked, from whom they feel far removed.

Jesus is filled with God and knows God intimately. What possibly could be added that would make a human being more divine, whatever exactly that means? After his death, God raises Jesus from the dead. The resurrection expresses God's complete approval and vindication of Jesus, as a father might vindicate his faithful and loving son. What could make Jesus more completely God's? Jesus lives now, with God, in all of us, breaking down the barriers that separate us from God and each other.

What else can be added to further deify Jesus, whatever.exactly that means?

For two millennia, Christians have tried to soar to heaven on the wings of answers that cannot bear weight. Foolishly, we have defined the exact nature of Jesus when we cannot ascertain our own. Pompously, we have explained his precise relationship to the Godhead without understanding God. Imprudently, we have answered how and whether Jesus is present in the bread and wine at our celebrations of his Last Supper by inventing words that science has demonstrated to be meaningless.

Unwilling to admit our ignorance, we have committed the unpardonable sin. We have arrogantly called ourselves right and denounced all other factions. Against the advice and will of Jesus, we have condemned, tortured, and slaughtered those who found answers different from our own. Now is the time to repudiate this dream of perfect understanding. We cannot get there from here. The only truth available to us is the lived truth. We can find it if we try to imitate the historical Jesus, here and now.

12 | *Imitate Jesus*

The righteous

The righteous are those who work hard, obey the law, and follow the rules. According to Jesus, people who consistently do these things risk overlooking the empire of God. The righteous are those who believe their group has the truth and the right way of doing things and all others are wrong. According to Jesus, people who believe these things are in grave danger of missing the empire of God. The righteous are those who think themselves superior to others because they have obeyed the rules and know the truth. According to Jesus, people who think themselves superior have missed the empire of God and possibly have rejected it as evil.

Jesus thinks the righteous must struggle to recognize their common humanity with others. The righteous may not have committed adultery, but they have lustful desires. They may not have stolen, but they are tempted by greed. Underneath our surface behavior, we are all much alike.

As a philosopher of biology, I agree wholeheartedly with this assessment. All sexually reproducing organisms have two fundamental needs, to garner resources and to reproduce. All people are sexually reproducing organisms. All need to garner resources and reproduce. The negative names for these needs are greed and lust. We all feel them. Evolution also makes us egocentric and worldly. Those people who lacked greed, lust, egocentricity, and worldly desires died out, leaving no offspring. The righteous and unrighteous have their basic needs and desires in common.

According to Jesus, the righteous must repent of their sense of being right and good. They must give up their conviction that they are so much more right and so much better than others, or they will overlook and/or reject the empire of God. There are two ways to repent of one's righteousness. The first is to acquire a healthy skepticism about one's own rectitude and that of one's group. The second is to look for truth and goodness in those who have different opinions and customs.

Philosophers cite three criteria for truth. The first is logical consistency. It is not logically consistent for Joseph and Mary to go from Bethlehem to Egypt to Nazareth, as they do in Matthew's Gospel and, on the same trip, travel from Nazareth to Bethlehem to Jerusalem and back to Nazareth, as they do in Luke's. By the criterion of logical consistency, at least one of these narratives is untrue.

The second criterion for truth is the correspondence of a sentence to what it expresses. For example, historians know that Luke's statement that Jesus is born when Quirinius is governor of Syria is false if Jesus is born in the reign of Herod the Great because the reigns do not overlap. This is everyone's common sense criterion for truth. If I speak the truth, I call it like it is.

The third criterion for truth is the fitting together (called consilience) of pieces in the big picture. For example, there is consilience between Darwin's theory of evolution, which demands much time for species to change, and geology's dating of the age of the earth at 4.5 billion years. There is consilience between Darwin's theory of common descent and the fact that all organisms have common DNA. A New Testament example might be the consilience between the Romans' elimination of rival emperors, their crucifying Jesus, and their thinking Jesus claimed to be an emperor.

To promote appropriate skepticism, people need only apply these criteria for truth rigorously to their own beliefs and statements and those of their group. Very few people or groups have a logically consistent set of beliefs or complete consistency between what they say and what they do.

Next, one might look for goodness and truth in other individuals and groups. Sometimes those who break the rules grow and mature in ways the righteous do not. They are like the yeast that makes the bread rise, yet is perceived as evil. Those who break the rules in order to help others may be better than the righteous who concentrate egocentrically on maintaining their own goodness.

Usually, the righteous are not very introspective. Their attachments are to external things. To become more introspective, they need to set aside quiet time for listening to God. During these quiet times, they might learn from the Pharisee's bad example and bring their weaknesses before God rather than their strengths. They need to examine the fear of chaos and need for structure that underlie their dependence on rules. In addition to awareness of their actions, they need to be attentive to their motives and desires. People who have never stolen anything may discover greed in other areas of their lives. They may be filled with jealous possessiveness toward their spouses and/or children. They may have exorbitant desires for higher status. They may covet their neighbor's swimming pool.

Spirituality that grows and matures into mystical union with God is difficult. It requires time set aside for listening to God. It demands a dedicated, disciplined, arduous, painful, slow journey. It takes tremendous courage. Yet most who try to find mystical union never attain it, for mystical union is a gift of God, not an acquisition. Those who think they are righteous because of a single experience of conversion need to contemplate the sufferings and strivings of the mystics who so thirst for God. They need to see their own smallness beside them. They might consider that Jesus, a religious genius, required thirty years to perceive the empire of God clearly.

Jesus says to search for the empire of God, to worship God with all our heart, mind, soul, and strength. For this, rules are not enough. For this, love is required. Love has a twin, freedom, for love cannot be coerced. Love is not jealous and does not strive for itself. It promotes freedom, and it promotes peace. Love, freedom, and peace stand opposed to the factionalism of the righteous.

The unrighteous

In Jesus' view, there are two types of the unrighteous. Both break the rules, but one sins, whereas the other does not. Most of the unrighteous are sinners who have pursued resources and reproduction to the extremes of greed, theft, adultery, and unwanted children. They need to be reminded that the rules are there for a purpose, that societies in which the social commandments are broken by the majority fall apart, that theft and murder harm people in all societies, and stable adult relationships are required for raising children well.

These unrighteous need to repent. Jesus tells them to do so. He is certain God will show mercy to those who repent. The repentant need to trust Jesus' assurance that God forgives them swiftly, readily, and without recrimination. Repentant sinners who learn to follow the rules have a further responsibility. Reformed into the righteous, they need to beware the temptations of righteousness.

The other category of the unrighteous is the category Jesus fits. Jesus breaks the rules but does not sin. He knows when love, liberation, healing, and revelation are more important than keeping rules, even significant ones. He realizes that those who keep all the rules all the time easily become filled with righteous arrogance, thereby paradoxically becoming the worst sinners.

To imitate Jesus through breaking the rules requires self-knowledge, moral sensitivity, heightened spirituality, and a ready willingness to repent. It also requires the ability to differentiate morally significant rules from mere conventions.

People who try to imitate Jesus by breaking rules that should be broken need guidelines for their behavior. In breaking rules, they can get confused and fall into sin, which is precisely what the righteous fear and warn against. The simplest guideline dates back to the ancient Greek physicians. It is "do no harm." This simple guideline can often clarify confusing cases. Beyond that, two more guidelines are useful. They are "do not exploit" and "do not be exploited." The latter is particularly important because those who do not adhere to rigid rules may have difficulty saying no, especially if they are compassionate.

These are the negative guidelines. The positive ones are already familiar. They are the heart of Jesus' message. Those who imitate Jesus are to promote forgiveness, love, freedom, and peace.

Rule breakers who do not run after sin are likely to be seekers after God. They are often more introspective than the righteous. However, they may be less self-disciplined. Like the righteous, they need to set aside time to listen to God, especially if they are about to break important rules.

Because they are introspective and flexible, seekers often find the pursuit of spirituality more attractive and easier than the righteous. Their prevailing danger is the pursuit of religion that is superficial, superstitious, and silly. In our culture, such religion often passes as new age spirituality. Serious seekers would do well to reach deeper. For those who want to imitate Jesus, scholarly study of the historical Jesus might suffice. Yet even here, caution is required. Scholarly study of Jesus can turn into an academic exercise applied neither to daily living nor to spirituality. This is a powerful danger for intellectuals, precisely those who will find the scholarly route attractive.

Most people need the support of a religious community. For those who want to imitate Jesus, this means a Christian community. Some factions of Christianity are closer to Jesus than others, but even those farthest from imitating Jesus cannot thwart him, for he is humble and available everywhere for those who seek him. The most sinful institutions cannot expel him. Nonetheless, seekers should approach the churches cautiously.

The churches

Many Christian churches rejoice in their righteousness and exclusiveness. They do not imitate Jesus. The two predominant western Christian traditions, Roman Catholicism and Protestantism, have taken different paths, so I will treat them separately, then add a few words about the eastern tradition known as Orthodoxy.

The Catholic Church declares itself infallible, with exclusive knowledge of the truth in faith and morals. In the past, it also claimed to have scientific and historical truth, but it has learned a few hard lessons and has retreated in every area where evidence might refute its claims. Faith and morals are not open to refutation by evidence, especially when Scripture is not considered decisive, as it is not for Catholicism. Thus, faith and morals are safe areas in which to claim infallibility. Only internal inconsistencies can show the church wrong on faith and morals. Some of its doctrines have developed inconsistencies over time, and they bring the church many theological twists and turns, but little soul searching.

The Catholic Church reveals the depths of the Pharisee's sin in Jesus' parable of the Pharisee and the tax collector. Convinced of his rightness, the Pharisee never asks whether he is wrong. Convinced of its rightness, the Catholic Church never questions itself. It can never uncover its own sins and repent, and it will stubbornly reject all outside efforts to disclose them. Jesus repeatedly condemns such dangerous arrogance. If the Catholic

Church wants to imitate Jesus, it must give up infallibility. If its individual members want to imitate Jesus, they must give up their need for an infallible church and receive the church's declarations critically. Many Catholics find that idea frightening. To imitate Jesus requires courage.

The Catholic Church has closed communion. It is an exclusive club. Jesus was inclusive. He ate with sinners and talked with Samaritans. If the Catholic Church wants to imitate Jesus, it must open its communion to others and welcome them, as Jesus did and does. Individual Catholics should break this sinful rule. So should non-Catholics.

The Catholic Church is a hierarchy of self-proclaimed goodness and rightness. It considers the lowly lay person less spiritual and more prone to error than the parish priest, which is why the lay person must obey the priest. But the parish priest himself is lowly and prone to error, too, compared to the priest in a religious order. (I correctly say *him*self. The Catholic Church says women are unworthy of the exaltation ordination brings. This means they are always the lowliest Catholics.) Bishops are not so lowly and error prone except when compared to Cardinals. Cardinals are even less lowly and less prone to error than bishops. At the top is the infallible Pope, who, since 1870, never errs in matters of faith and morals pronounced *ex cathedra.*

Such a hierarchy of self-proclaimed goodness and rightness turns Jesus' life and teachings upside down. Jesus raised up the lowly. The Catholic Church keeps the lowly in their places. Jesus was egalitarian. The Catholic Church is hierarchical. Jesus preached against self-righteous arrogance. The Catholic Church has built arrogance and self-righteousness into its structure. The Catholic Church is not the mythological anti-Christ of Protestant legend, but it is certainly anti-Jesus. If the Catholic Church is to imitate Jesus, it must dismantle its hierarchy. Individual Catholics need to protest this institutionalized travesty of Jesus' teachings. Especially harmed are women who suffer from constant individual, spiritual, and organizational discrimination. A general strike by all women who volunteer in the church, work for it, or give it money might get some results. Smaller measures will not do much, for great power will be necessary to pierce the church's thick armor of arrogance.

Protestantism protested against the Catholic Church early in the sixteenth century CE. It cast off the authority of the Pope and leveled the hierarchy through its doctrine of the priesthood of all believers. It rejected tradition and most rituals, proclaiming Scripture as sole authority. The exception was the Church of England, now known as the Anglican Communion, which includes the American Episcopal Church. It, too, rejected the Papacy, but it called early traditions authoritative and also invoked reason. Its embrace of the authority of reason helped it weather the later storms of science and biblical criticism better than either the Catholic or more Protestant churches.

Protestantism began as a faction, and factionalism is its besetting sin. Lacking any authority but Scripture and calling upon all Christians to interpret Scripture for themselves, it finds itself in a position similar to that of Judaism during the two first centuries. Charismatic leaders collect followers and establish new factions. Each faction insists that it knows the best way and fights the others over petty and unknowable doctrinal details often masquerading as significant theological issues. Any church proclaiming it has exclusive access to truth or the sole correct interpretation of Scripture is arrogant and self-deluded. Those who want to imitate Jesus should go elsewhere.

John Calvin (1509-1564) believed all people are totally and irrevocably sinful. God elects some to save and damns the rest. Because all are equally sinful in God's sight, election is arbitrary. Calvin's God holds a wrinkled nose while blindly plucking an undeserving few from perdition. Calvinists fail to realize that our desires for resources and reproduction are good, necessary for life, and part of God's plan. They cease to be good only when excessive and exploitative.

Calvin's doctrines are an embarrassment to Jesus. Jesus says God forgives sins and loves us like a caring father. Jesus' God has standards of judgment, showing mercy to the repentant and justice to the righteous. Calvinist churches that want to imitate Jesus need to revise these doctrines. Members who try to imitate Jesus should protest if these doctrines are preached and withhold funds if they continue to be preached, or walk out and look for a church that imitates Jesus more closely.

If they want to imitate Jesus, churches preaching a God of hell-fire need to change their message. Jesus taught and lived a God of mercy who forgives all who ask. The barrier to forgiveness is not divine wrath, but human blindness and arrogance. The unforgiven are the righteous who reject God's acceptance of sinners and God's open invitation to join the banquet of the liberated.

Many Protestant churches emphasize sudden, complete conversions. They are following Luke's portrait of Paul in Acts (9:3-6). Sudden conversions are dramatic, fun, and sometimes lasting. They may herald the beginning of a maturing spiritual and moral life, but they may not. They are not the same as spirituality, and they do not confer it. Spirituality requires a life of dedicated self-discipline, countless hours listening for God, and increasing sensitivity to God's presence and will. Conversions, like prophets, are known by their fruits (Matt 7:20). Churches using conversion experiences to exclude some from the congregation or from full participation in the life of the church are not imitating Jesus.

Catholicism claims to be the church Jesus established through Peter. Protestantism claims antiquity through its embrace of Scripture as the sole source of authority. Yet the oldest churches were the Greek-speaking assemblies whose Scripture was the Septuagint. The Orthodox Church, Christianity's eastern tradition, sprang from these Greek-speaking assemblies and later formed national churches in Eastern Europe and Russia. The Orthodox Church still uses the Septuagint. It emphasizes mysticism and human communion with the divine. Authority in it is diffused among Scripture, early theologians and councils, and later Orthodox leaders. It has not split into warring factions. In all these matters, it seems close to Jesus. Yet it has closed communion and a hierarchical priesthood. More fatally, it lacks any authoritative source like the Catholic concept of ongoing revelation through the Pope or the Anglican resort to reason to help it cope with science and biblical criticism. Its predominance in less-developed areas and its repression under communism have exacerbated the problem. Whether it will be able to remake itself so it can survive in the new century is an open question.

By ancient tradition, the Catholic and Orthodox Churches build blockades against outsiders. Protestant churches erect barriers among themselves, often over wholly trivial differences. All construct doctrinal fortifications. Blockades, barriers, and fortifications are the metaphors of war, exclusion, and isolation. Jesus speaks in metaphors of peace, love, and freedom. He wants us to live by them.

The larger society

We live in a society that thrives on competition, status seeking, and acquisition. These are worldly values Jesus rejects. They exclude. They create hierarchies. They make possessions a criterion of worth. They indulge a religiosity that is silly, superficial, and superstitious. They are too busy to join God's gracious banquet. Those in this society who wish to imitate Jesus need to drop out of the race.

Martin Luther (1483-1546) throws light on this suggestion. He was once a monk, but left the monastery and married to live in the larger society. He argues that people can live holy, spiritually fulfilling lives in and through the larger society. Through their diverse occupations and stations in life, Christians can fulfill the Christian vocation to love God and neighbor. I think Luther is right. To live God-centered lives does not entail joining a monastery or a commune or going back to the land. It merely requires a person set aside worldly values in imitation of Jesus.

For a young person, setting aside worldly values means choosing an occupation in which worldly values do not have priority. There are many such occupations, from lowly jobs where worldliness is not expected to the helping professions like nurse, doctor, social worker, counselor, and teacher. Creative professions like engineer, museum curator, author, and artist are also possibilities. Many lawyers, too, avoid the worldly profession of corporate law and enter domestic or constitutional law or work for a variety of aid agencies. These lawyers might not be as rich as corporate lawyers, but Jesus does not recommend the pursuit of riches. A six thousand square foot house, a pool, a tennis court, and a three-car garage are not necessary for happiness unless a person has adopted worldly values contrary to Jesus.

To imitate Jesus is to emphasize simplicity in clothing and other possessions. People who practice simplicity are rich without wealth, for they limit their desires and do not run after baubles. If they acquire wealth, they rejoice in the generosity that it allows them to express toward others. Simplicity is a valuable antidote to competitive acquisitiveness.

Jesus protested social structures that keep the poor in poverty. Those who imitate him need to protest them, too. As a guideline, they need to encourage the larger society to put its energies and money into public goods of benefit to all, like libraries, museums, schools, public transportation, and health care. They might work for affordable housing in their communities. In the nation, they might support inheritance taxes on the rich, the graduated income tax, livable wages at the bottom of the scale and limited benefits at the top.

Jesus was inclusive. To imitate him, people need to resign from exclusive clubs and move out of gated communities. Those who live simply do not envy such lifestyles. Inclusiveness in a democracy means creating a voting system where everyone's vote counts equally.

Jesus wanted factions and nations to cease fighting. He sought peace. Everyone can vote for peace. The military industrial complex will lose power if voters cease voting for senators who get military contracts in their states for equipment the military does not even want. Everyone can work for peace by supporting peaceful organizations financially. Those who have time can volunteer in such organizations and become mediators. To promote literacy and birth control is to work for peace, too.

There are hundreds of ways in the twenty-first century, in church and out of church, for the righteous and the unrighteous to imitate Jesus. Each way someone adopts enhances the quality of life for all, making it more loving, peaceful, and free. To imitate Jesus is wonderfully fulfilling.

Conclusion

Christianity goes wrong about two weeks after Jesus' disciples believe he is resurrected. It goes wrong in the Holy Land as his Jewish disciples equate the resurrected Jesus with the Messiah figure in Daniel 7, then with the earthly Messiah figure of David. It goes wrong in the Greek and Roman cities and towns as his Gentile disciples think of him as the true emperor who has ascended to the gods, and as they equate that figure with the *logos*, the creative word and wisdom of God.

When these concepts are attached to Jesus, they invert his message. They turn Jesus into the savior of the world and a sacrifice for sin. In stark contrast, Jesus' message is that people do not need a savior, and salvation does not require sacrifice. God is present and available, here and now, and forgives the sins of those who ask, without priestly mediation and without sacrifice. Those who are unforgiven, who receive justice rather than mercy, are the righteous who do not want to be forgiven because they think they have no need of forgiveness. Thinking themselves justified, they long for justice for themselves and condemnation for their enemies. Jesus speaks harshly against their arrogance and hatred and condemns their dream of victory and revenge at the end time.

What we can do now about Christianity's error is to turn to the historical Jesus and imitate him. In terms of worship, this means giving up the concept of the imperial God who has the trappings of an oriental despot with a throne and a retinue of angels and who practices militant revenge against enemies. This distant God inspires fear and the rites and rituals that accompany fear. Such a God does not inspire action in the world. With such a God, religion becomes set apart, removed from daily life.

Against the imperial concept of God stands Jesus' concept. Jesus sees God as intimate, nearer to us than our own hearts. His God is always present and always forgives those who ask. His God inspires humility by being close, available, and forgiving. His God loves, liberates, heals, and reveals, bringing peace. Worshipers who experience God's intimacy become humble about their own goodness and knowledge, for next to God, they know they are ignorant and sinful. The intellectual face of humility is skepticism. People who experience God's intimacy realize that all concepts of God are inadequate and doctrines are dust. This helps them work for love, freedom, and peace for all instead of victory for their own faction.

A church that worships Jesus' God will be a humble church, filled with members who know they are not righteous and do not have the truth. It will be a simple church in which the New Testament is read more than the Hebrew Scriptures. It will be a church that experiences God's presence, here and now, and God's forgiveness. It will be a church that lives to serve others. If you find such a church, join it gratefully and serve.

Imitators of Jesus will live in the world but not be worldly. They will be much like the church they seek—humble, simple, and skeptical, meeting God in everyday life and serving others. They will worship Jesus by imitation. What better worship could you possibly offer?

WORKS CONSULTED

General Reference

Achtemeier, Paul J., (ed.), 1985: *Harper's Bible Dictionary*, HarperSanFrancisco, San Francisco.
Barrett, David B. et al. (eds.), 2001: *World Christian Encyclopedia: A Comparative Survey of Churches and Religions in the Modern World*, Oxford University Press, Oxford.
Bullinger, Ethelbert W., 1975: *A Critical Lexicon and Concordance to the English and Greek New Testament*, Zondervan, Grand Rapids, Michigan.
Cross, F. L. and E. A. Livingstone (eds.), 1997: *The Oxford Dictionary of the Christian Church*, Oxford University Press, London.
Day, A. Colin, 1992: *Roget's Thesaurus of the Bible*, HarperSanFrancisco, San Francisco.
Edwards, Paul (ed.). 1967: *The Encyclopedia of Philosophy*, Macmillan Publishing Co., New York.
Ferguson, Everett (ed.), 1990: *Encyclopedia of Early Christianity*, Garland Publishing, Inc., New York.
Laymon, Charles M. (ed.), 1971: *The Interpreter's One-Volume Commentary on the Bible*, Abingdon, Nashville, Tennesee.
Mays, James L. (ed.), 1988: *Harper's Bible Commentary*, HarperSanFrancisco, San Francisco.
Meeks, Wayne A. (ed.), 1989: *The HarperCollins Study Bible*,

New Revised Standard Version, HarperCollins, New York.
United Bible Society, 1990: *The New Greek-English Interlinear New Testament*, Tyndale House Publishers, Inc., Wheaton, Illinois.

Historical Jesus

Allison, Dale, 1996: "The Eschatological Jesus: Did He Believe the End Was Near?" *Bible Review* **12**, 34-41, 54-55.
Borg, Marcus J., 1994: *Jesus in Contemporary Scholarship*, Trinity Press International, Valley Forge, Pennsylvania.
Borg, Marcus J., 1994: *Meeting Jesus Again for the First Time: The Historical Jesus and the Heart of Contemporary Faith*, HarperSanFrancisco, San Francisco.
Carroll, John T. and Joel B. Green, 1995: *The Death of Jesus in Early Christianity*, Hendrickson, New York.
Chilton, Bruce, 1994: "The Eucharist—Exploring Its Origins," *Bible Review* **10**, 36-43.
Crossan, John Dominic, 1991: *The Historical Jesus: The Life of a Mediterranean Peasant*, HarperSanFrancisco, San Francisco.
Daly, Robert J. 1978: *Christian Sacrifice: The Judeo-Christian Background before Origen*, Catholic University of America Press, Washington, D. C.
Dunn, James D. G., 1988: "Pharisees, Sinners, and Jesus" in Jacob Neusner, et al. (eds.), *The Social World of Formative Christianity and Judaism*, Fortress Press, Philadelphia, pp. 264-289.
Eisenman, Robert, 1997: *James the Brother of Jesus: The Key to Unlocking the Secrets of Early Christianity and the Dead Sea Scrolls*, Viking, New York.
Ehrman, Bart D., 1999: *Jesus: Apocalyptic Prophet of the New Millennium*, Oxford University Press, Oxford.
Fredriksen, Paula, 1988: *From Jesus to Christ: The Origins of the*

New Testament Images of Jesus, Yale University Press, New Haven, Connecticut.

Fredriksen, Paula, 1999: *Jesus of Nazareth, King of the Jews: A Jewish Life and the Emergence of Christianity,* Alfred A. Knopf, New York.

Funk, Robert W. and the Jesus Seminar, 1993: *The Five Gospels: The Search for the Authentic Words of Jesus,* HarperSanFrancisco, San Francisco.

Funk, Robert W. and the Jesus Seminar, 1998: *The Acts of Jesus: The Search for the Authentic Deeds of Jesus,* HarperSanFrancisco, San Francisco.

Hengel, Martin, 1977: *Crucifixion in the Ancient World and the Folly of the Message of the Cross,* Fortress Press, Philadelphia.

Jeremias, Joachim, 1966: *The Eucharistic Words of Jesus* (tr. Norman Perrin), SCM Press, London.

Johnson, Luke T., 1995: "The Search for (the Wrong) Jesus," *Bible Review* **11**, 20-25, 44.

Josephus, Falvius, 1981: *The Compete Works of Josephus* (tr. William Whiston), Kregel Publications, Grand Rapids, Michigan.

Meier, John P., 1991: *A Marginal Jew: Rethinking the Historical Jesus, Volume 1: Roots of the Problem and the Person,* Doubleday, New York

Meier, John P., 1994: *A Marginal Jew: Rethinking the Historical Jesus, Volume 2: Mentor, Message, and Miracles,* Doubleday, New York.

Mason, Steve, 2000: "Where Was Jesus Born?" *Bible Review* **16**, 31-39, 51-53.

Murphy, Federick J. 1991: *The Religious World of Jesus: An Introduction to Second Temple Palestinian Judaism,* Abingdon Press, Nashville, Tennessee.

Sanders, E. P., 1985: *Jesus and Judaism,* SCM Press, London.

Sanders, E. P., 1993: *The Historical Figure of Jesus,* Penguin Books, London.

Spong, John Shelby, 1994: *Resurrection, Myth or Reality: A Bishop's Search for the Origins of Christianity*. HarperSanFrancisco, San Francisco.

Stahl-Pollat, Geraldine and Bruce Chilton, 1995: "Jesus Chose a New Symbol," in "Readers Reply," *Bible Review* **11,** 45-46.

Vermes, Geza, 1973: *Jesus the Jew: A Historian's Reading of the Gospels,* Collins, London.

Wise, Michael, Martin Abegg, Jr., and Edward Cook, 1996: *The Dead Sea Scrolls: A New Translation,* HarperSanFrancisco, San Francisco.

Wright, N. T., 1996, "How Jesus Saw Himself," *Bible Review* **12**, 22-29.

The Two First Centuries

Ferguson, Everett, 1993: *Backgrounds of Early Christianity* (second edition), William B. Eerdmans Publishing Company, Grand Rapids, Michigan.

Horsley, Richard A. (ed.), 1977: *Paul and Empire: Religion and Power in Roman Imperial Society*, Trinity Press International, Harrisburg, Pennsylvania.

Neuser, Jacob, 1982: "Scripture and Mishnah: Authority and Selectivity" in Frederick E. Greenspahn (ed.), *Scripture in the Jewish and Christian Traditions: Authority, Interpretation, Relevance*, Abingdon, Nashville, pp. 65-85.

Pearson, Birger A., 1997: *The Emergence of the Christian Religion: Essays on Early Christianity,* Trinity Press International, Harrisburg, Pennsylvania.

Price, S.R.F., 1984: *Rituals and Power: The Roman Imperial Cult in Asia Minor*, Cambridge University Press, Cambridge.

Schafer, Peter, 1997: *Judeophobia: Attitudes toward the Jews in the Ancient World,* Harvard University Press, Cambridge.

Schmidt, Thomas, 1997: "Jesus' Triumphal March to Crucifixion: The Sacred Way as Roman Procession," *Bible Review,* **13,** 30-37.

Schowalter, Daniel N., 1993: *The Emperor and the Gods: Images from the Time of Trajan,* Fortress Press, Minneapolis.

Segal, Alan F., 1990: *Paul the Convert: The Apostolate and Apostasy of Saul the Pharisee,* New Haven, Yale University Press.

Shanks, Hershel (ed.), 1999: *Ancient Israel: From Abraham to the Roman Destruction of the Temple,* Prentice Hall and the Biblical Archaeology Society, Washington, D.C., and Upper Saddle River, New Jersey.

Taylor, Lily Ross, 1931: *The Divinity of the Roman Emperor,* Scholars Press, Middletown, Connecticut.

Wright, N. T., 1999: "Paul's Gospel and Caesar's Empire," *Reflections* **2,** 42-65.

Wright, N. T., 2000: "Paul, Leader of a Jewish Revolution," *Bible Review* **16,** 8.

Mysticism/Mind-Body Problem

Underhill, Evelyn, [1911] 1990: *Mysticism: The Preeminent Study in the Nature and Development of Spiritual Consciousness,* Doubleday, New York.

McGinn, Colin, 1999: *The Mysterious Flame: Concious Minds in a Material World,* Basic Books, New York.

Kellehear, Allan, 1996: *Experiences Near Death: Beyond Medicine and Religion,* Oxford University Press, New York.

Moody, Raymond A., Jr., 1975: *Life after Life: The Investigation of a Phenomenon—Survival of Bodily Death,* Bantan Books, New York.

Ring, Kenneth, 1980: *Life at Death: A Scientific Investigation of the Near-Death Experience,* Coward, McCann and Geoghegan, New York.

Jesus and Buddha

Borg, Marcus (ed.): *Jesus and Buddha: The Parallel Sayings.* Seastone, Berkeley, California.

Borg, Marcus and Ray Riegert, 1999: "East Meets West: The Uncanny Parallels in the Lives of Buddha and Jesus." *Bible Review* **15**, 16-29, 50.

Evolution

Darwin, Charles [1859] 1964: *On the Origin of Species,* Harvard University Press, Cambridge, Massachusetts.

Mayr, Ernst, 1982: *The Growth of Biological Thought: Diversity, Evolution, and Inheritance,* Harvard University Press, Cambridge, Massachusetts.

Williams, Patricia A., 2001: *Doing without Adam and Eve: Sociobiology and Original Sin,* Fortress Press, Minneapolis.

Human Violence

Keeley, Lawrence H, 1996: *War before Civilization,* Oxford University Press, New York.

Index Entries

A

B

C

D

E

F

G

H

I

J

K

L

M

N

O

P

Q

R

S

T

U

V

W

Y

Z